THE ULTIMATE UNOFFICIAL
ENCYCLOPEDIA
FOR
MINECRAFTERS
AQUATIC

THE ULTIMATE UNOFFICIAL
ENCYCLOPEDIA
FOR
MINECRAFTERS
AQUATIC

AN A-Z GUIDE TO THE MYSTERIES OF THE DEEP
MEGAN MILLER

Sky Pony Press
New York

Copyright © 2019 by Hollan Publishing, Inc.
Minecraft® is a registered trademark of Notch Development AB.
The Minecraft game is copyright © Mojang AB.

Sky Pony Press books may be purchased in bulk at special discounts for sales promotion, corporate gifts, fund-raising, or educational purposes. Special editions can also be created to specifications. For details, contact the Special Sales Department, Sky Pony Press, 307 West 36th Street, 11th Floor, New York, NY 10018 or info@skyhorsepublishing.com.

Sky Pony® is a registered trademark of Skyhorse Publishing, Inc.®, a Delaware corporation.

Minecraft® is a registered trademark of Notch Development AB.
The Minecraft game is copyright © Mojang AB.

Visit our website at www.skyponypress.com.

10 9 8 7 6 5 4 3 2

Library of Congress Cataloging-in-Publication Data is available on file.

Cover design by Brian Peterson
Cover art by Megan Miller

Print ISBN: 978-1-5107-4727-2
Ebook ISBN: 978-1-5107-4738-8

Printed in China

FOREWORD

This encyclopedia of all things Aquatic is a celebration of the amazing underwater world of Minecraft. The ocean has grown from its early incarnation as a dark expanse populated only by squid to an amazing world of dolphins, coral reefs, treasure, ships, ruins, and more. (If, like many players, you've been a landlubbing Minecrafter, this encyclopedia will give you the details you need to know to conquer the oceans. Plus, it is also an essential read for planning any water world challenges in Minecraft!)

While this book is written for the Java Edition of Minecraft (Java Edition 1.13/1.14), it does include references to elements that are different in the Bedrock Edition. The notation JE is used when a feature is found (currently, as of this writing) in the Java Edition of Minecraft. Similarly, the notation BE indicates a feature found only in the Bedrock Edition. However, as the game develops, the Bedrock Edition and Java Edition features are growing more and more in sync, and the bulk of the game features are identical in both versions.

ACHIEVEMENTS, AQUATIC

The Achievement system in the Bedrock Edition of Minecraft is a series of more than 90 goals to complete in-game. They are designed to introduce new players to the features in Minecraft as well as encourage players to take on the most difficult challenges, like killing a Wither. The current list of aquatic-related achievements in Bedrock include:

Ahoy!: The in-game description is: "Find a shipwreck."

Alternative Fuel: "Power a furnace with a kelp block."

Atlantis?: "Find an underwater ruin."

Castaway: "Eat nothing but dried kelp for three in-game days."

The Deep End: "Defeat an elder guardian."

Do a Barrel Roll!: "Use Riptide to give yourself a boost."

When you complete an achievement in the Bedrock Edition, the Achievements entry changes from black and white to color.

Dry Spell: "Dry a sponge in a furnace."

Echolocation: "Feed a dolphin fish and have it lure you to treasure."

Free Diver: "Stay underwater for two minutes."

Let It Go!: "Using the Frost Walker boots, walk on at least one block of frozen water in a deep ocean."

Marine Biologist: "Use a bucket on any fish mob to collect it."

Me Gold: "Dig up a buried treasure."

Moskstraumen: "Activate a conduit."

One Pickle, Two Pickle, Sea Pickle, Four: "Place four sea pickles in a group."

Sail the 7 Seas: "Visit all ocean biomes."

Sleep with the Fishes: "Spend a day underwater."

Moskstraumen

Moskstraumen is a word used in Nordic countries (Scandinavia, Norway, etc.) that means "maelstrom." There is also a famous ocean area of strong, dangerous whirlpools and swirling currents off the coast of Norway called the Moskstraumen.

ADVANCEMENTS, AQUATIC

Advancements are a system of challenges in the Java Edition of Minecraft that you complete as you play. They guide the player through the different areas and activities in Minecraft. In the Bedrock Edition, these are called Achievements. There are currently just four aquatic-related advancements to achieve in the Minecraft advancement system; for two you'll need a trident, for the other two you'll be catching fish. They are:

Advancements

Catch a fish... without a fishing rod!

Tactical Fishing

Roll over an icon in the Java Edition Advancements tab to see the advancement title and description.

A Throwaway Joke (Adventure tab): The in-game explanation is: "Throw a trident at something." Don't throw it at a block of grass or some cobblestone; throw it at a mob—even a passive one will do!

Very Very Frightening (Adventure tab): "Strike a villager with lightning." To do this, you'll want to enchant your trident with Channeling. Channeling summons a lightning bolt to the target victim, and a lightning strike changes some mobs to their evil counterparts. Creepers evolve into the even more deadly charged creepers, villagers transform into witches, and a struck pig becomes a zombie pigman.

Fishy Business (Husbandry tab): "Catch a fish." Use a fishing rod to catch any fish.

Tactical Fishing (Husbandry tab): "Catch a fish . . . without a fishing rod!" Get yourself a bucket of water, and right-click it on a fish to capture it live in the bucket.

Note: To reveal the Adventure tab, you'll want to kill or be killed by any mob. To reveal the Husbandry tab, just eat something!

ANEMONE

The anemone is one of the twenty-two tropical fish in Minecraft that are named for (and colored like) real-life tropical fish. In Minecraft, the anemone is colored as an orange-gray stripey.

In real life, the anemonefish, also called clownfish, are a family of about thirty species of small fish. Anemonefish are known for having a close relationship with (and are named for) another animal, the sea anemone.

The sea anemone is a relative of coral that looks like a plant, with waving tentacles that are often venomous. Anemonefish hide among the sea anemone's tentacles, and are immune to the tentacle's stings. The two animals have a symbiotic relationship, and each protects the other from certain kinds of predators. Anemonefish also help bring small fish to the sea anemone for its food, and can eat leftover tidbits. Anemonefish are often colored with oranges and reds, some with yellows and blacks. They often have a white stripe.

See also: Clownfish, Tomato Clownfish, Tropical Fish.

AQUARIUMS

Aquariums (and stocked fishponds) aren't added by themselves to Minecraft, but the ability to create them is there. You can pick up any fish, live, with water buckets, and transport them to an enclosed area of water. Right-click your bucket into the aquarium's water to add your fish. There's no limit to the size or shape of your aquarium, as long as you fill it with water to keep the fish alive.

See also: Bucket of Fish, Project: Build an Aquarium.

Build an in-ground aquarium or fishpond with seagrass, sea pickles, kelp, lily pads, and buckets of tropical fish.

PROJECT: BUILD AN AQUARIUM!

This aquarium uses glass panes for its walls. There will be an air space between the aquarium water and the panes, but this is easily covered by using full blocks at the aquarium wall corners and slabs above the pane tops. Fish may swim into the air gap and seem stuck, but they can swim back into the main water. A benefit of this is that when they are in the air gap, they are especially bright and visible!

What You'll Need

- 15 sand blocks
- 20 blocks of prismarine brick (or other solid decorative block for the base)
- 48 quartz blocks

- 44 dirt blocks (temporary)
- 16 buckets of water
- 44 glass panes
- 3 coral blocks of one color
- 1 coral block of a second color
- 2 kelp
- 12 sea pickles
- 2–3 coral of different colors
- 4–6 coral fans of different colors
- 4–7 seagrass
- 20 quartz slabs
- 5 or more tropical fish in buckets

Step by Step

1. Place a 3x5 block rectangle of sand that will be the bottom of your aquarium.

2. Add a border of prismarine brick or other decorative block around the sand.

3. On top of the back border, build the back of the aquarium with a wall of quartz seven blocks long and four blocks high. This quartz backing will brighten up the interior and make it a bit easier to see your fish.

4. Build up two pillars of quartz, four blocks high, on the two front corners of the base.

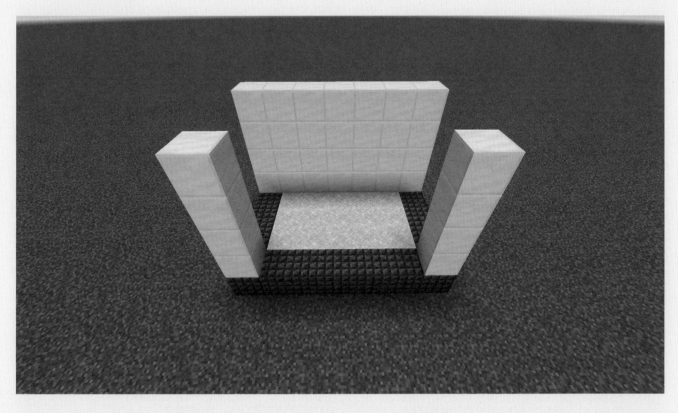

Note: Now we're going to build temporary walls with dirt, fill the aquarium with water, and then install the glass pane walls. Using dirt as temporary walls helps in filling the aquarium with water. It stops you from accidentally placing water in the same block as a glass pane, because the water will waterlog the glass pane and flow outside of the aquarium area. (If this does happen at any point, replace the waterlogged glass pane with a solid block, then break the solid block and replace it with a glass pane.)

5. Place a row of dirt above the front and sides of the aquarium as shown.

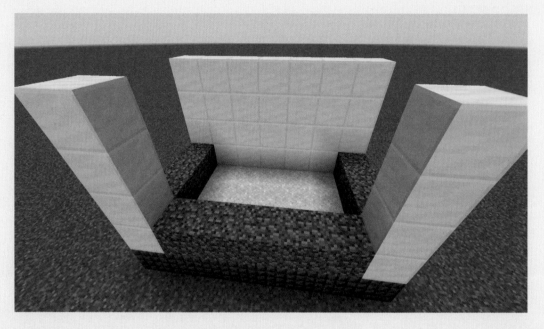

6. Place three buckets of water along the bottom of the back wall, leaving a space between each placement. Place one bucket of water at the right front corner. The red Xs show where to place these. When you are done, you should have 15 water source blocks of water now, none flowing.

7. Add another layer of dirt above the bottom row of dirt.

8. Place four buckets of water in the same places as you did in step 6, just one block up. Again, you should have a full layer of non-flowing water source blocks between the walls.

9. Repeat steps 7 and 8, twice, by adding a third, then a fourth level of dirt to the temporary walls, filling each in with water as you did in step 8.

10. Now replace each dirt block with a glass pane. Glass panes are easiest to place when you place them on or against a block, so start at the top and work down.

11. Now it's time to decorate! Add a pillar of three coral blocks at the back, and a few blocks away place the other single coral block.

12. Add a couple kelp plants to the bottom and place your sea pickles in several locations (up to four on a block) to light up the water. Add a few coral on the sandy bottom and coral fans on the sides or tops of the coral blocks. Fill in any empty sand block tops with seagrass.

13. Finish your aquarium walls by placing a row of quartz slabs at the tops of the four walls of your aquarium.

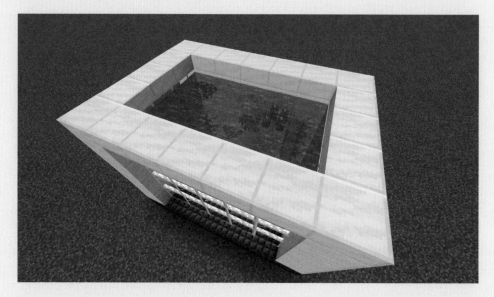

14. When you have finished decorating, place your tropical fish. Make sure not to place them against the glass blocks, or you will break the air gap and have to replace the wall. To be safe, place them against the center of the back quartz wall.

AQUATIC UPDATE

Before the 1.13 Aquatic Update, Minecraft's oceans were mostly desolate stretches of water. There were squid and guardians in ocean monuments, but that was pretty much it. The Aquatic Update added a host of new blocks, items, mobs, and features, mostly ocean related or ocean dwelling, including:

Blocks

Multiple types of coral blocks, corals, coral fans, including dead coral, kelp, dried kelp blocks, seagrass, sea pickles, conduit, turtle eggs, blue ice, bubble columns, buttons, pressure plates, and trapdoor variants for the different types of wood, wood (bark on all sides) (JE), stripped logs, slabs and stairs for prismarine,

The Update Aquatic (JE 1.13) brought the ocean to life with new mobs, fish, items, coral reefs, and more.

dark prismarine, and prismarine brick

Biomes

Cold, Lukewarm, and Warm variants of Ocean, Deep Frozen Ocean Biome, New End biomes: Barren Islands, Floating, Medium, and High

Mobs

Dolphin, drowned, fish (cod, pufferfish, salmon, and tropical fish), phantom, turtle

Items

Arrow of Slow Falling, arrow of the Turtle Master, buried treasure explorer map, debug stick (JE), dried kelp, fish buckets, heart of the sea, nautilus shell, phantom membrane, scute, trident, turtle shell

Status Effects

Conduit Power, Dolphin's Grace (JE), Slow Falling

Enchantments

Channeling, Impaling, Loyalty, Riptide

Structures

Buried treasure, coral reefs, icebergs, shipwrecks, underwater caves and ravines, underwater ruins

Potions

Potion of Slow Falling, potion of the Turtle Master
See also: Resource Checklist.

ARROW OF THE TURTLE MASTER

The arrow of the Turtle Master is a type of tipped arrow. It imparts the effects of Slowness and Resistance to its victim. As with any tipped arrow, the effect lasts an eighth of the normal potion's duration. To create arrows of the Turtle Master, combine one lingering[1] potion of the Turtle Master surrounded by eight regular arrows in a crafting table.

See also: Potion of the Turtle Master.

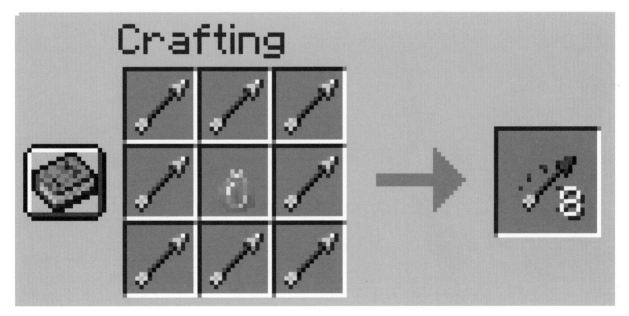

Craft eight arrows of the Turtle Master with a lingering potion of the Turtle Master and eight arrows.

---

1   A lingering potion is created by brewing a bottle of dragon's breath into a splash potion.

BEACH

The Beach Biome is a narrow stretch of sandy land found along coastlines at the edges of ocean biomes. The sand at the water's edge slopes smoothly into the water; underwater you'll also find clay, dirt, and gravel blocks. Beneath the sand itself you will find sandstone, similar to deserts; the sandstone prevents sand from falling into any caves below. The turtle is the only passive mob that can spawn on beaches. Sugar cane is the one plant that grows at the water's edge of beaches.

See also: Stone Shore Biome, Snowy Beach Biome.

BIOMES

The scientific meaning of the word *biome* is used to refer to the collection of flora and fauna that live in a particular environment. These environments are often also categorized by rainfall, temperature, and humidity, among

The Beach Biome generates between land biomes and ocean biomes.

other factors. Different scientists, over time, have categorized Earth biomes in slightly different ways.

In Minecraft, biomes are similar to the general scientific biomes: Each biome has a specific range of temperatures, may or may not have rainfall, and may spawn mobs or plants unique to that biome. Many Minecraft biomes are named for biome types established by biologists, such as Taiga, Desert, Tundra, and Savanna. Overall, Minecraft has five primary categories of in-game biomes:

Minecraft's land biomes range in topographical height and geography, temperature, humidity, and flora and fauna. Sky, leaf, and grass colors also change with the biome.

1. **Snowy:** Snowy Tundra and two variants, Ice Spikes and Snowy Mountains.
2. **Cold:** Mountains (and variants like Gravelly Mountains), Taiga (and variants like Giant Spruce Taiga), and Stone Shore.
3. **Medium/Lush:** Plains, Forest, Swamp, Jungle, River, Beach, Mushroom Fields, Mushroom Fields Shore, and the End, along with variants.
4. **Dry/Warm:** Desert, Savanna, Badlands, the Nether, and variants.
5. **Aquatic:** Warm Ocean, Lukewarm Ocean, Ocean, Cold Ocean, Frozen Ocean, and variants.

Minecraft's aquatic biomes consist of ten ocean biomes, each individualized by different temperatures and the types of flora and fauna it supports.

See also: Biomes, Aquatic.

> ### Flora and Fauna
> *Flora and fauna* is a term used to describe the natural plant species (flora) and animal species (fauna) that live in a geographical area.
> The term *biota* is used when other types of living organisms like fungi are included.

BIOMES, AQUATIC

Minecraft's ocean biomes are large bodies of water, ranging from hundreds to thousands of blocks wide. Oceans reach a water surface level of y=63, and their depths range from around fifteen blocks deep (ocean floor at around y=45) to about thirty (ocean floor at around y=32) in Deep Ocean variants.

There are five ocean temperature levels and two deepness levels, and these combine to make a total of ten ocean biomes: Warm and Deep Warm Oceans, Lukewarm and Deep Lukewarm Oceans, Oceans and

You can see where a warmer ocean biome meets a colder ocean biome by the change in color.

Deep Oceans, Cold and Deep Cold Oceans, and Frozen and Deep Frozen Oceans. The ten biomes vary also in terms of water color, flora (seagrass, sea pickles, kelp), fauna (fish, dolphins, drowned, squid, guardians, elder guardians), and generated structures (ocean monuments, shipwrecks, underwater ruins, coral reefs). Ocean monuments spawn only in Deep Ocean variants.

Ocean floors are typically gravel, with some patches of clay, dirt, or sand, and can feature underwater ravines and caves. The floor rises and falls, with some hills rising up to the surface as islands. You will also find bubble columns in oceans, created by magma blocks, which can pull a swimmer or boat underwater.

In addition to the ocean biomes, there are a few other "watery" biomes, like River and Beach. These aren't included in the game's definition of aquatic biomes, but are in this book!

See also: Biomes, Ocean, Ocean Floor, and individual entries for Beach, Cold Ocean, Frozen Ocean, Frozen River, Lukewarm Ocean, Mushroom Field Shore, River, Snowy Beach, Stone Shore, Swamps, and Warm Ocean.

BLACK TANG

The black tang is one of Minecraft's common tropical fish named for a real-life fish. It uses the gray flopper color and pattern.

In real life, the black tang is entirely black and is one of the rarest of the tang fish. Tangs in general are sometimes called doctorfish, surgeonfish, or unicornfish, because of the sharp, knife-like spines near their tail fins, which they can use against their enemies.

See also: Blue Tang, Yellow Tang, Tropical Fish.

BLUE ICE

Blue ice is one of the three types of ice in Minecraft (excluding the magical and temporary Frosted Ice that is produced by Frost Walker-enchanted boots.) You can find it in Frozen Ocean

Blue ice naturally generates in clumps in Frozen Ocean Biomes.

Biomes, at the bottom of icebergs, or in standalone clumps or outgrowths. You can also craft blue ice with nine blocks of packed ice. Blue ice is even more slippery than packed ice and doesn't melt when it is near torches or other light sources. Traveling by boat on blue ice is currently the fastest way to travel in Minecraft.

See also: Ice, Frozen Ocean.

BLUE TANG/BLUE DORY

The blue tang is one of Minecraft's named tropical fish and uses the gray-blue flopper color and pattern scheme.

In real life, the blue tang is a member of a family of tropical fish called tangs, surgeonfishes (or doctorfishes), and unicornfishes, known for sharp spines by their tail, used for defense.

The blue dory tropical fish is found only in the Bedrock Edition, and appears to be the counterpart to the Java Edition's blue tang, as the blue tang doesn't appear in the Bedrock Edition. The famous animated film fish, Dory, is a blue tang tropical fish. The Bedrock Edition blue dory uses the Minecraft gray-sky sunstreak pattern.

See also: Black Tang, Yellow Tang, Tropical Fish.

BOATS

Besides swimming, boats are the de facto transport of aquatic Minecraft. They've been a part of Minecraft since the Java Edition Alpha and have been continually under improvement. Gone are the days when boats broke at the mere sight of a lily pad. Today, boats have paddles,

Top, blue tang (JE); Bottom, blue dory.

fit two, and on ice offer the fastest travel speeds in Minecraft. (On water, they are about as fast as minecarts.) Other great things about boats include:

- If you fall while you are in a boat, you usually will not take any damage.
- When you're in a boat, your hunger level stays the same.
- You can catch mobs in boats—they won't leave the boat by themselves. This means boats are great for catching and transporting villagers and mobs.

Fun fact: Boats are entities in Minecraft because they are moving objects. That means they have health (about 2 hearts) and their health even regenerates.

See also: Swimming.

BREATHING UNDERWATER

When you slip below the water surface, your heads-up display (HUD) will show a new status line for your oxygen level. This is your oxygen bar, a row of ten bubbles. Your oxygen level (and number of bubbles) will decrease the longer you stay underwater. Once you have no oxygen left (after about fifteen seconds), you will start taking drowning damage at one heart per second.

There are several ways to keep breathing and avoid drowning while you are swimming underwater.

See also: Drowning, Underwater Survival.

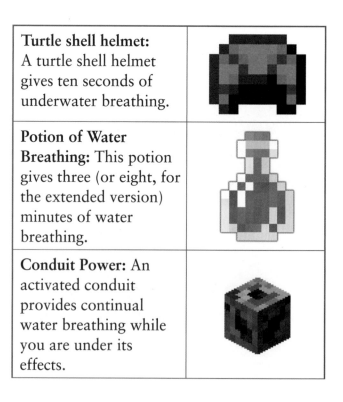

Turtle shell helmet: A turtle shell helmet gives ten seconds of underwater breathing.	
Potion of Water Breathing: This potion gives three (or eight, for the extended version) minutes of water breathing.	
Conduit Power: An activated conduit provides continual water breathing while you are under its effects.	

Respiration enchantment: A helmet enchanted with Respiration will give you an increased time to breathe underwater.	
Bubble column: You can refresh your oxygen levels in a bubble column.	
Sponge: You can use a dry sponge to soak up dozens of blocks of water around you and create a breathing space. Depending on where you are, the water remaining around you will usually fill in again, quickly.	
Doors, banners, gates (JE): Place one of these to create a pocket of space to get oxygen in an emergency. Be careful in placing these, however, as you'll need a two-block space for placing them. The gate will need to be at the top of a two-block-high space to create the air at your head level. A banner only creates the air pocket in its upper half.	

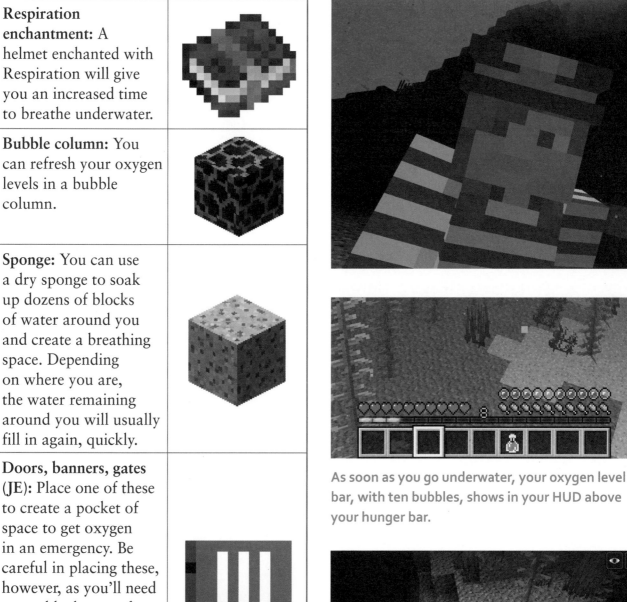

As soon as you go underwater, your oxygen level bar, with ten bubbles, shows in your HUD above your hunger bar.

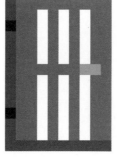

Placing a door creates two blocks of air you can breathe while underwater.

BUBBLE COLUMNS

Bubble columns are created when magma blocks or soul sand blocks are placed in water, with only source water blocks above. Either of these blocks will generate a 1x1 block wide column of bubbles above it that can either push or pull objects at about fifteen blocks per second. Magma blocks generate a whirlpool bubble column, which can pull entities and items down. If you are in a boat over a whirlpool column, your boat will start shaking violently, and you can be pulled down if you don't get out of the whirlpool quickly.

Soul sand blocks generate an upward bubble column and can push mobs and items to the surface. The higher a bubble column reaches, the faster the object goes, and the column can even throw the player up out of the water by about a block. The appearance of a bubble column indicates that an underwater ruin or ravine lies below. A ravine might have a dozen bubble columns where lava at its depth has turned to magma.

You can use a bubble column to quickly regenerate your oxygen level. Another popular use for bubble columns is for transport systems and player elevators.

See also: Project: Bubble Column Elevator.

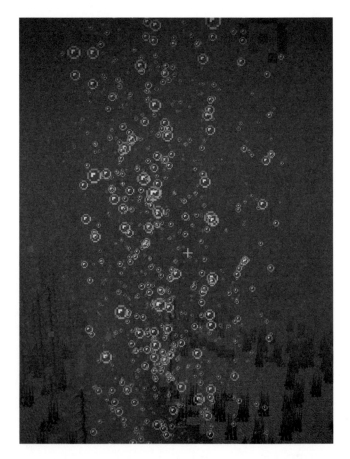

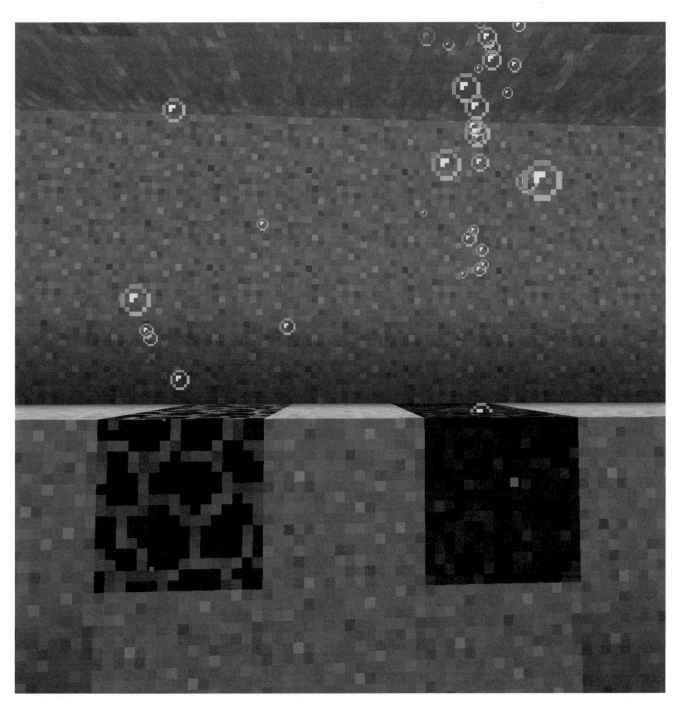

Magma blocks create a bubble column that pulls objects down to it; soul sand bubble columns push objects to the surface.

PROJECT: BUBBLE COLUMN ELEVATOR

Bubble columns are an amazingly fast way to move up and down in Minecraft. You can easily make elevators to get up and down from the tops of mountains or high cliffs and move quickly between the levels of your base. The up elevator uses soul sand to push you up, and the down elevator uses a magma block to pull you down.

This elevator uses light blue blocks to indicate the Going Up elevator and lime green blocks for the Going Down side. You can use whichever blocks you like and construct the platforms as large or small as you like.

What You'll Need

- 17 prismarine brick blocks for the central column
- 54 light blue glass blocks for three walls of the up elevator, including the bottom entrance
- 54 lime green glass blocks for three walls of the down elevator, including the bottom exit
- 6 signs
- 1 dirt block (temporary)
- 2 buckets of water
- 2–3 temporary or dirt blocks

- 2 kelp
- 1 soul sand block
- 1 magma blocks
- Additional decorative blocks for the top and bottom levels (I've used an additional eight prismarine brick blocks, twenty-five light blue concrete blocks, and twenty-five lime green concrete blocks.)

Step by Step

1. Place the central prismarine brick block that will be the center column for the elevators. This will be the back wall for the two elevators.

2. On one side, place the two side walls for the "Going Up" side of the bottom level using four light blue glass blocks. The blue color will help indicate that this is the Up side.

3. On the opposite side, place four lime green glass blocks as side walls for the "Coming Down" part of the bottom level. The green color will indicate that this is the Down side.

4. Build these bottom level walls to be three blocks high.

5. On the "Going Up" side, place three signs on the outer blocks of one wall, as shown.

6. Do the same for the "Coming Down" side of the bottom level.

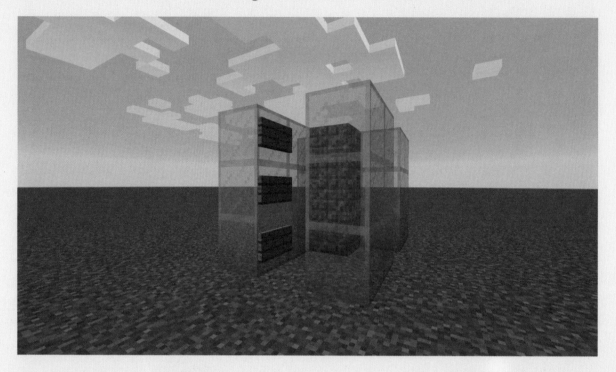

7. Place a temporary dirt block between the outer glass blocks at the top of the "Going Up" side. This is to help you place a block in the next step.

8. Place three glass blocks and one prismarine brick block as shown to be the base of the walls of the enclosed "Going Up" elevator.

9. Remove the temporary dirt block.

10. Now do the same on the "Coming Down" side of the elevator: First, place a temporary dirt block on one outer glass block.

11. Add three glass blocks to form the base of the outer and side walls of the elevator and remove the dirt block.

12. Build up the walls of the two elevators to the level you want. I've added fourteen block levels to make the entire elevator seventeen blocks high.

13. Build out a platform at the top of the elevators. Use your additional decorative blocks. I've used lime concrete for the Down side and light blue concrete for the Up side, and prismarine brick between the sides.

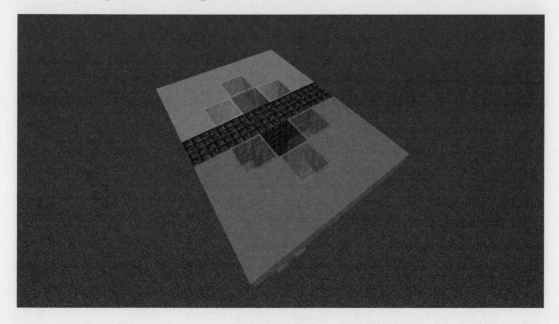

14. Place one bucket of water at the tops of each of the two elevator sides. This water will flow down the length of each elevator tunnel.

15. At the bottom level of each of the elevators, make sure the bottom block is grass or dirt. Plant kelp on the bottom block. Do this on both sides.

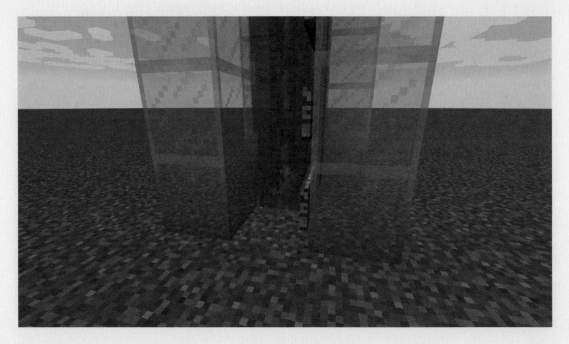

16. Now, you can wait for the kelp to grow to the top water block in each elevator, or manually place kelp all the way to the top. As the kelp grows into each flowing water block above it, the water block changes into a source block. (The bubble columns only work with source blocks.)

17. Once the kelp has grown to the top, return to the bottom level and break the kelp stalk. Do this on each side.

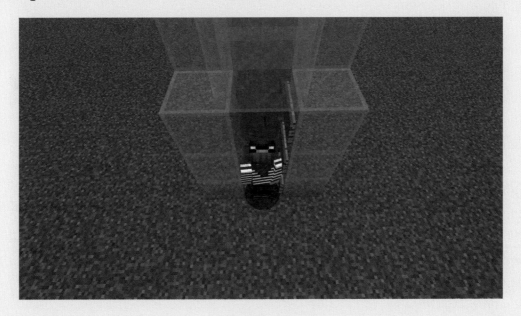

18. On the Going Up side, replace the bottom block of the elevator with a block of soul sand. You will see bubbles start to rise from it.

19. On the Coming Down side, replace the bottom block of the elevator with a magma block. Here you'll see bubbles begin to flow down to the magma block.

20. Finish the bottom layer with decorative blocks as you like. I've used lime concrete for the Coming Down side and light blue concrete for the Going Up side.

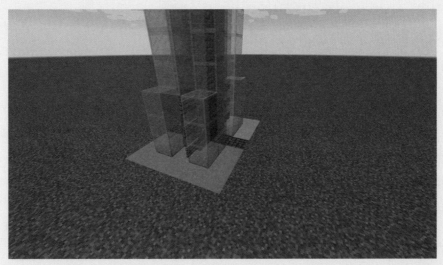

21. Check out your elevator! Step into the blue Going Up side. It goes fast and you'll even bounce into the air a bit! Move out onto the platform when you arrive. Drop into the green Down side. Press forward as you get to the bottom, so you can hop out of the elevator before spending much time if any on the magma block. (If you find yourself stuck on a magma block, press Shift, or sneak, to avoid taking damage.)

BUCKET OF FISH

Fill a bucket with water, right-click it on a swimming fish mob, and you'll have a bucket of (one) fish. Right-click your bucket of fish to release it along with the water. There are four "types" of buckets of fish: bucket of cod, bucket of salmon, bucket of pufferfish, and bucket of tropical fish. When you pick up a tropical fish, the bucket in your inventory will show what type of fish you have: if its one of the twenty-two named fish, like a black tang, you'll see its name. If it is one of the thousands of other patterns of tropical fish, it will show its pattern and colors, like "glitter, blue." However, the icon for the item bucket of tropical fish always shows a clownfish.

TIP: To name a live fish mob, place the bucket of that fish in an anvil and add the name. If you are collecting tropical varieties, this can help you keep track of and identify what you've caught so far.

See also: Tropical Fish, Fish.

BURIED TREASURE

Buried treasure is a randomly generated loot chest found in beaches and more rarely underwater on the floor of the ocean. The chest is usually buried or covered by a block of sand or gravel, but sometimes stone or ore. You can find buried treasure by

using buried treasure maps, which are found in shipwreck map chests and underwater ruins chests.

The types of loot you can find in a buried treasure chest include hearts of the sea, diamonds, emeralds, iron, gold, prismarine crystals, iron swords, leather tunics, TNT, cooked cod, and salmon. Additionally, in the Bedrock Edition, you have a chance to find chainmail armor, leads, name tags, music discs, cake, potions of Water Breathing and Regeneration, books and quills, and bottles o' enchanting.

See also: Buried Treasure Map, Shipwrecks, Underwater Ruins.

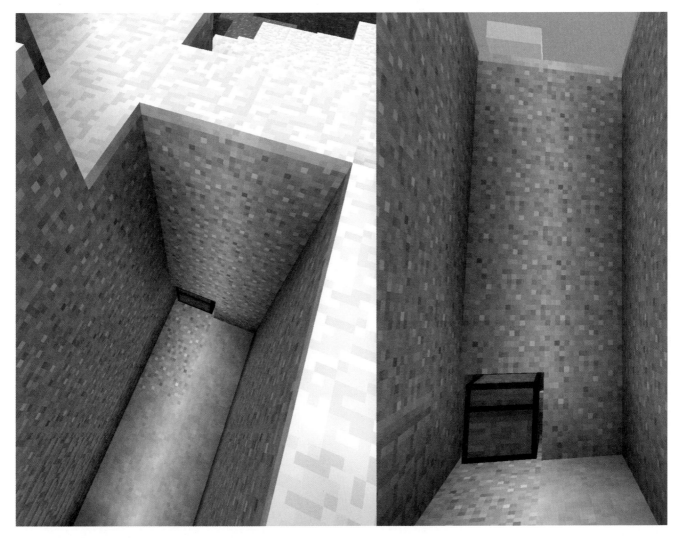

Buried treasure chests may be more than a few blocks beneath the surface.

BURIED TREASURE MAP

The buried treasure map is a type of explorer map. It shows where single chests of loot are buried in the Minecraft world, along ocean beaches and coastlines. You find them in shipwreck map chests and in chests of underwater ruins. As with any explorer map, a buried treasure map shows the general area and layout of the treasure's location and a white marker indicates where you are. If you're unsure about how to use an explorer map, see the entry Explorer Map.

Even with a map, finding buried treasure can be difficult. The red cross covering the treasure is big, and the map doesn't give you exact coordinates, so it's easy to dig near the loot chest, but not near enough. To get as close to the treasure as possible, try to match your white marker so that the tip just projects from the bottom of the red X.

If you find map chests that are near each other (for example, an underwater ruin chest near a shipwreck map chest), the maps will often point to the same treasure. So to find more treasure, travel further!

See also: Explorer Map, Shipwrecks, Underwater Ruins, Buried Treasure.

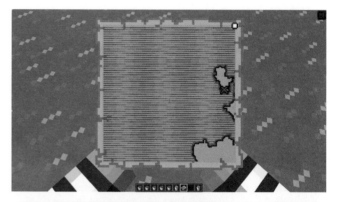

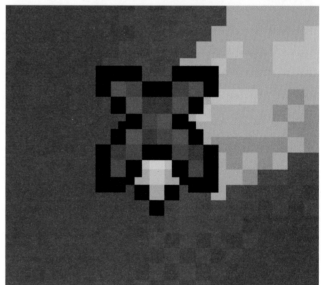

To get close to the buried treasure, position the white marker showing your location right under the red X so that the tip is just pointing out.

East South North West

To find your direction, use the sun, which always moves from east to west. Look at the sun so that your cursor is at the bottom edge of the sun. Wait a moment, and whichever way the sun is moving points to the west. To double-check, face in that west direction and make sure that the sun is going down.

BUTTERFLYFISH

The butterflyfish (or in BE, butterfly fish) is one of Minecraft's tropical fishes named for a real-life fish. In Minecraft's color and pattern scheme, it is a white-gray brinely (see page 157).

IRL (In Real Life): Butterflyfish are a group of more than 100 tropical fish that live in coral reefs; many are known for being brilliantly colored and patterned with hues of red, orange, yellow, blue, black, and white.

See also: Ornate Butterflyfish, Tropical Fish.

CHANNELING

Channeling is an enchantment that can only be used on the trident, and has only one level. A Channeling trident will call forth a bolt of lightning that strikes your target as it is also hit by the trident. The lightning strike will change creepers into charged creepers, pigs into zombie pigmen, and villagers into witches. This spectacular attack will only happen on dry land open to the sky and during thunderstorms.

The Channeling enchantment cannot be used with the Riptide enchantment.

See also: Riptide, Trident.

CICHLID

The cichlid is one of Minecraft's twenty-two named tropical fish. In Minecraft's color and pattern scheme, it is a blue-gray sunstreak. In real life, cichlids are a very large group of more than 1,500 species of fish, including food fish like tilapia and colorful tropical fish. The cichlid family of fish shares a unique jaw structure that distinguishes them from other fish.

See also: Red Cichlid, Tropical Fish.

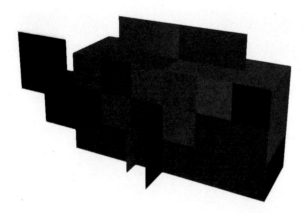

CLAY

Clay is one of the four main blocks that form the ocean floor, along with gravel, sand, and dirt. It's also found at the bottoms and sides of swamps, lakes, and rivers.

You'll find patches of clay usually closer to the surface and borders of oceans, and by beaches and islands where sand also is found. When you break clay, you'll get four balls of clay, which you can craft back, four at a time, into blocks. If you smelt clay balls, you'll get bricks that can be crafted into brick blocks or flowerpots. If you smelt clay blocks, you'll get terra-cotta building blocks. You can dye the terra-cotta to make stained terra-cotta blocks, and then further smelt these stained blocks to get colorfully patterned glazed terra-cotta.

CLOWNFISH

The clownfish is one of Minecraft's tropical fish named for a real-life fish. In Minecraft's color and pattern scheme, it is an orange-white kob (see page 157). In real life, they're a type of anemonefish, a bright orange color with white stripes. They are known for being born male, with the ability to change into females.

See also: Anemone, Tomato Clownfish, Tropical Fish.

COD

Cod is one of the four types of fish mobs in Minecraft, along with salmon, tropical fish, and pufferfish. They're found in any ocean biome except Warm Ocean and Frozen Ocean biomes. They are spawned in groups of four to seven fish and will swim in schools of up to nine cod. Cod can be eaten raw or smelted for a very nutritious in-game food.

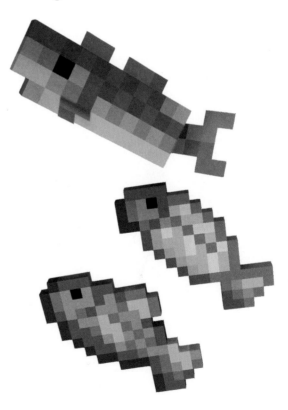

Top to bottom: The mob cod, the raw cod item, and the cooked cod item.

In real life, cod are a common ocean fish popular as food and as a source of cod liver oil, which contains a variety of important nutrients and vitamins.

See also: Fish.

COLD OCEAN

The Cold Ocean Biome has brilliant deep blue surface waters. You can find kelp, seagrass, ruins, and shipwrecks here. Mobs that spawn underwater in the Cold Ocean Biome are cod, dolphins, drowned, salmon, and squid. The Deep Cold Ocean Biome is about twice as deep, allowing ocean monuments to spawn, with their guardians and elder guardians.

A Deep Cold Ocean Biome, deep enough for an ocean monument to spawn.

CONDUIT

A conduit is a special block—a block entity—that you use to create Conduit Power. You craft it from eight nautilus shells around one heart of the sea. You can use any tool to break it, although a pick is fastest. Conduits give off a light level of fifteen.

Conduits are used to produce Conduit Power, and to do so must be activated. To activate a conduit, you must place it in water and surround it with a specially configured frame of blocks. The full frame consists of three overlapping 5x5 square "rings," each centered around one of the three axes (x, y, and z) of the conduit. The only blocks that can be used for the frame are prismarine, prismarine brick, dark prismarine, and sea lanterns. The entire frame uses forty-two blocks, and this will activate Conduit Power for a range of ninety-six blocks in all directions.

However, you don't need a full frame to activate the conduit. You just need a minimum of sixteen blocks of the frame filled in, and for each seven blocks added to the frame, Conduit Power will extend another sixteen blocks from the conduit. This means that for fourteen blocks of frame (not activated until sixteen are placed), the

To activate a conduit, you must place three rings of prismarine or sea lanterns around it.

Conduit Power range will be thirty-two blocks. With twenty-one blocks filled in, the range will be forty-eight blocks; with twenty-eight blocks the range is sixty-four blocks, and so on.

A fully framed, activated conduit will also deal damage to any nearby hostile mobs at a rate of four health (two hearts) every two seconds. Again, this only works if the mobs are in water or rain.

Placed in water, a conduit attracts particles that look like tiny hearts of the sea with eyes. When a conduit

An activated conduit opens up to show a reddish "eye" at its center and attracts tiny particles that look like miniature hearts of the sea.

Block Entity

Block entities are blocks that have more properties or abilities than ordinary blocks like cobblestone. They don't always use the cube model of an ordinary block. Block entities include banners, beds, brewing stands, cauldrons, chests, flowerpots, furnaces, monster spawners, redstone comparators, and signs, among others.

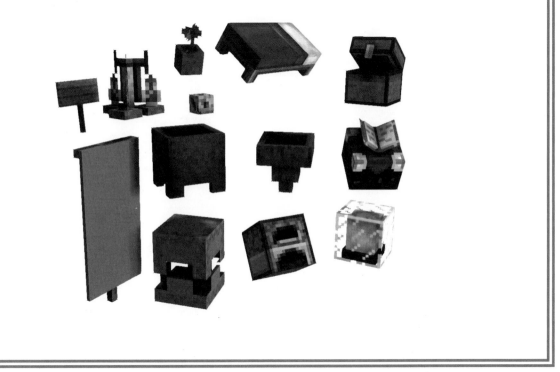

activates, it opens and slowly bobs up and down, its tiny frame twisting around a heart of the sea at its center. The conduit makes a humming sound combined with a beating heart sound. When a conduit is fully activated, with a forty-two-block frame, the heart of the sea shows a pupil of orange and red and looks more like an eye.

See also: Conduit Power

CONDUIT POWER

Activated conduits produce a combination of special effects called Conduit Power. Conduit Power gives players the effects of Water Breathing, Night Vision, and Haste while they are within range of the activated conduit. Conduit Power only works when a player is in water (or rain).

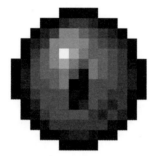

See also: Conduit

CORAL

Coral are one of the three types of Minecraft blocks that make up coral reefs, along with coral blocks and coral fans. Although coral in real life are animals, in Minecraft they look like and are similar to ferns or flowers, being non-solid or transparent blocks with a non-cube shape. There are five types of coral: brain coral, bubble coral, fire coral, horn coral, and tube coral. Each has a slightly different shape and color, but all can only grow or be placed on the top of blocks. You can only gather coral with a Silk Touch enchanted tool; otherwise, it will disappear when broken.

If you place coral outside of water it will "die" within a moment, turning

Live and dead tube coral.

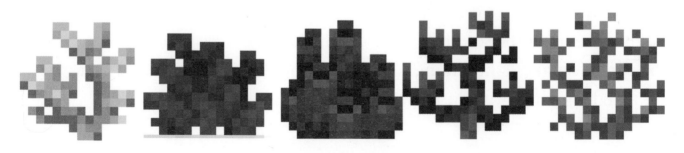

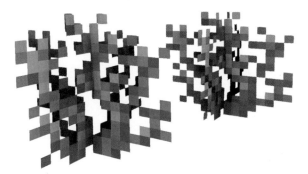

Brain coral.

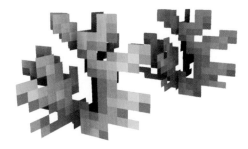

Horn coral.

Bubble coral.

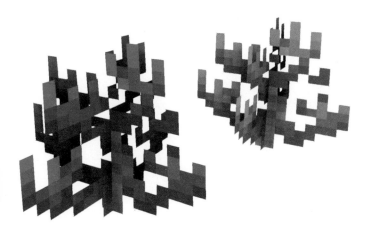

Fire coral.

into gray dead coral. You can place it above water and keep it alive as long as one side of it is touching water. One way to do this is to put a slab on the upper half of a block of water (so the slab is now "waterlogged") and then place the coral on top of this slab.

You can also grow coral in Warm Ocean Biomes by using bone meal on dirt, gravel, or sand. Bone mealing the warm ocean floor will produce sea-grass as well.

CORAL BLOCKS

Coral blocks are solid blocks of coral that generate in coral structures, forming coral reefs. They come in the same five varieties as coral and coral fans: brain, bubble, fire, horn, and tube. They will die (turn gray) if they are broken with a pick that is not enchanted with Silk Touch, or if they are placed without at least one side touching water.

See also: Coral Fans, Coral.

Coral blocks compared with their "dead" counterparts. From left to right: tube coral, brain coral, bubble coral, fire coral, horn coral.

CORAL FANS

Coral fans, like coral, are non-solid blocks that are generated in Minecraft as part of coral reef structures. They come in the same five variants as coral and coral block and have the same coloring as their coral and coral block counterparts. They can grow or be placed on the sides and tops of blocks. On the sides of blocks, they take a fan-like shape, and on the tops of blocks, the fans spread out into a flattened shape. They behave in all other circumstances like coral, and they can only be broken with Silk Touch picks. They will die unless at least one side is touching water.

See also: Coral.

From left to right, side and top versions of fire, horn, bubble, tube, and brain coral.

CORAL REEFS

Coral reefs are structures resembling real coral reefs, and generate in random configurations in Warm Ocean Biomes. They're composed of multiple configurations of coral blocks, coral, and coral fans, some branching like trees, others in blocky clumps. Sea pickles and seagrass grow on and around coral. Tropical fish and pufferfish spawn here, swimming in small groups around the reefs. Coral reefs can be small, consisting of just a few clumps of coral structures, or range up to hundreds of blocks in either direction.

Each type of coral has five variants: brain coral, bubble coral, fire coral, horn coral, and tube coral. These correspond to real-world types of coral. There are no real-world "blocks" of coral, but some coral does have a fan-like appearance.

See also: Coral, Coral Blocks, Coral Fans.

COTTON CANDY BETTA

The cotton candy betta is one of Minecraft's twenty-two tropical fish that are based on real-life fish. In Minecraft's color and pattern scheme, it is a rose-sky spotty. In real life, this fish is part of the betta family of fish, many of which have spectacular coloring and fins. Bettas with iridescent blue and pink colorings are often referred to as "Cotton Candy" bettas.

See also: Tropical Fish.

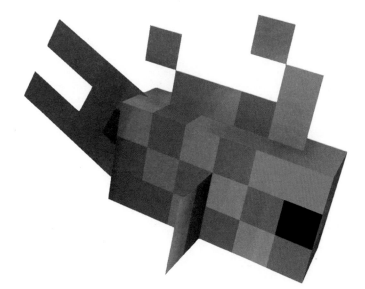

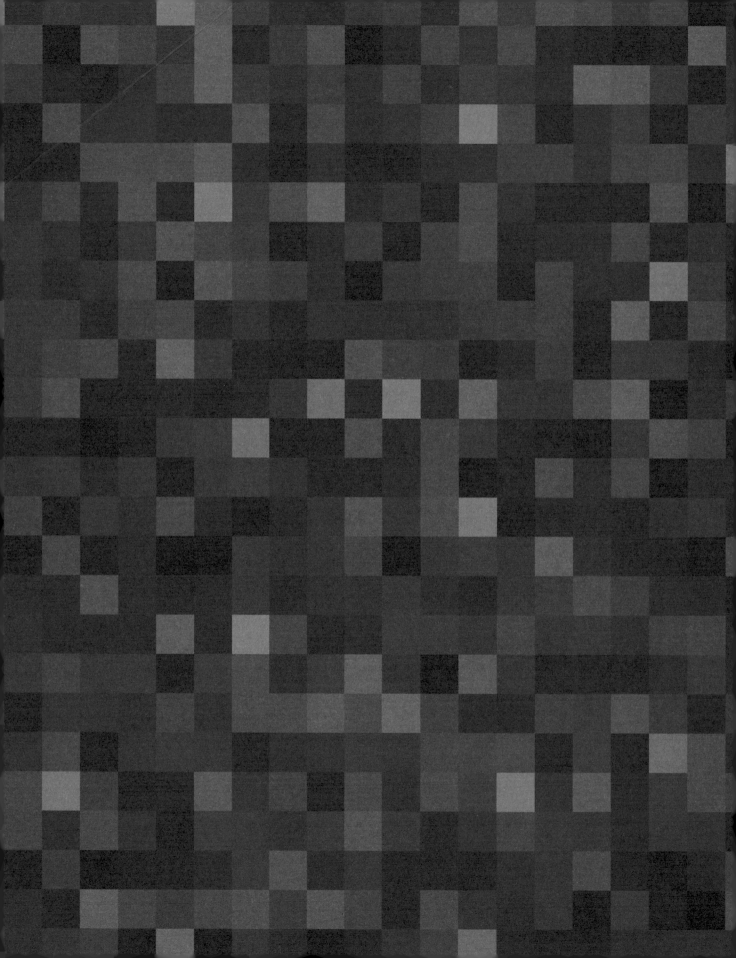

DARK PRISMARINE

Dark prismarine is one of three prismarine blocks in Minecraft, along with prismarine and prismarine bricks. All three are building blocks used to create ocean monuments found in Deep Oceans, and along with sea lanterns, one of the four blocks that can be used to activate a conduit. Of the three prismarine blocks, dark prismarine is the rarest, used in a few details and to cover the gold blocks hidden in the monument. However, you can craft dark prismarine blocks with eight prismarine shards surrounding one ink sac. Dark prismarine is also craftable into dark prismarine slabs and stairs.

See also: Prismarine, Prismarine Shards.

DIRT

Dirt is one of the main blocks that make up the ocean floor, although it typically is found in patches near coastlines and islands.

DOLPHIN

Dolphins are one of the most complicated mobs in Minecraft, having a number of different activities and interactions. They're a neutral mob,* attacking only when attacked, and spawn regularly, like squid, in all ocean biomes but frozen ones. They're designed to behave playfully, like dolphins in real life. You'll find them typically in groups, swimming together and leaping playfully out of the water, and they will chase after swimming players and players in boats. If you drop an item near them—any item, like a paper item or a torch—they will nose and toss the item between each other. Swimming near a dolphin will give you the effect Dolphin's Grace, allowing you to swim much faster for five seconds. Because dolphins like to closely follow swimming players, you can get the effect continually while you swim together.

Feed a dolphin raw cod or salmon and it will guide you to the nearest sunken treasure chest hidden in abandoned underwater ruins or a shipwreck! If you break that chest, the

dolphin can then find the next nearest shipwreck or ruins with a treasure chest.

Like their real-life counterparts, dolphins do need to occasionally breathe air and will drown if underwater for several minutes. On the other hand, they also need water to live: if they are out of water for several minutes, they'll begin to suffocate. They will look for the nearest water and jump toward it.

You can hurt or kill a dolphin, but like villagers and baby animals, they

DOLPHIN STATS

Type: Neutral
Spawns: Warm through Cold Ocean Biomes
Health: 10 HP
XP: 0
Damage Hard mode: 4 HP
Damage Normal mode: 3 HP
Damage Easy mode: 2 HP
Damage from spikes: 2 HP
Drops: Raw cod
Rare drops: None

* Neutral mobs only attack if they are attacked or provoked first; otherwise, they are passive.

will drop no experience orbs for you. They may drop one or two raw cod, but that's it. If you strike them, you will provoke them into hostility, and nearby dolphins will join together to attack you back.

Dolphins will leap out of the water and chase items that you throw.

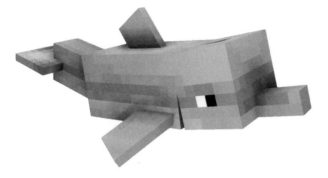

DOLPHIN'S GRACE

Dolphin's Grace is a status effect granted to a player swimming near a dolphin. It boosts the player's swimming speed considerably for five seconds (up to eighty blocks per second according to the official Wikipedia!).

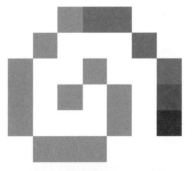

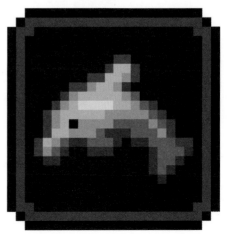

BOX: Status Effect

A status effect is a special condition or ability, either beneficial or harmful, granted to a player or mob in the game. Potions grant status effects, like Underwater Breathing, and so can activated beacons or conduits, cave spider attacks, and eating zombie flesh. Status effects include Absorption, Conduit Power, Fire Resistance, Haste, Nausea, and Poison, among others. When you are under the influence of a status effect, you'll give off swirly particles. Different effects have differently colored particles. You will also see a status effect icon at the top right of your screen and when you look at your inventory.

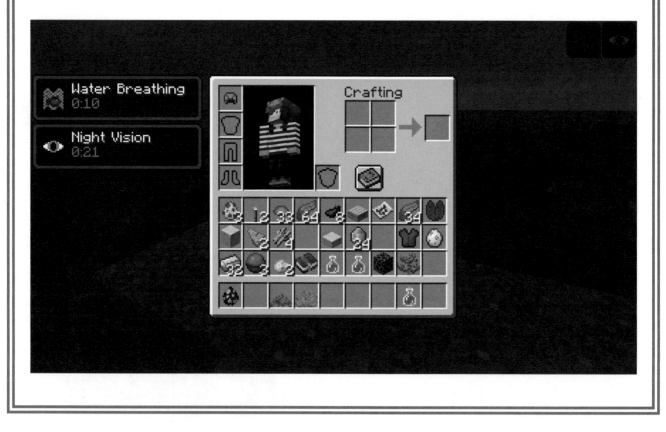

DOTTYBACK

The dottyback is one of the twenty-two tropical fish in Minecraft that are named for (and colored like) real-life tropical fish. In real life, the dottyback (Pseudochromis) are a family of more than 100 species of small tropical fish. They are often brightly colored in combinations of magenta, yellow, purple, red, orange, and blue. The Minecraft dottyback uses the tropical fish blockfish pattern and the plum and yellow colors, making it a plum-yellow blockfish.

See also: Tropical Fish.

DRIED KELP

Dried kelp is an item that comes from smelting kelp in a furnace. It is food and gives a player a half haunch of hunger (one hunger point), making it a very easy and quick source of food early in the game.

You can craft nine dried kelp into a dried kelp block, which isn't edible but is now a valuable fuel for furnaces, as one block can smelt twenty items. And if you're hungry, you can craft a single dried kelp block back into nine dried kelp for eating!

DROWNED

The drowned is the zombie of the dark waters. Although it has the same health and melee strength as a regular zombie, it can be much more dangerous! They'll spawn in the ocean at light levels below seven, so daytime won't help you. They can swim, moving faster than a regular zombie floating above water. And about 15 percent of drowned will spawn with a trident, a spear-like weapon that it can throw directly at you and give you a full nine points of damage (4.5 hearts!).

Unusually, during the day, a drowned that is out of water and prevented from going to water will become passive. In the water, during the day, the drowned stay on the ocean floor, swimming to attack only players underwater. At night, however, they will rise to the surface to chase their victims and may climb onto land. If the drowned get up onto land at night when the sun cannot burn them, they are a menace to villagers and iron golems like regular zombies. They are also an enemy of turtles. They will chase baby turtles and stomp on turtle eggs.

Keep a lookout for any basic zombies taking a dip in the ocean: If a regular zombie (not a zombie villager) is underwater for thirty seconds, it will shiver and shake for fifteen seconds and then transform into a drowned. The dry (non-moist) desert-dwelling zombie variant, the Husks, have a longer, double conversion process. Underwater, they first turn into a regular zombie (regular moistness) and then into a drowned (fully moist).

If you see a chicken floating by itself in the middle of the ocean, it is the sole survivor of a drowned chicken jockey: a baby drowned that spawned underwater riding on a chicken. The chicken floated to the top of the ocean, and the baby zombie on top burned to a crisp in the sun. You may find some zombie flesh floating around nearby!

DROWNED STATS

Type: Hostile

Spawns: Below sea level in light level 7 or below, in Warm through Cold Ocean Biomes

Health: 20 HP

XP (Adult): 5

XP (Baby): 12

Damage Hard mode: 4 HP

Damage Normal mode: 3 HP

Damage Easy mode: 2 HP

Damage from trident: 9 HP

Drops: Rotten flesh, gold ingots

Rare drops: Trident, fishing rod, nautilus shell

DROWNING

Drowning is one of the many ways in Minecraft to take damage. You have an oxygen bar with ten bubbles that appears on your HUD when you venture underwater. The bar decreases the longer you are underwater, and when it is empty, you begin to take damage from drowning, at about two HP a second.

Most mobs, if they are underwater, will try to reach the surface, and if they can't will drown. Mobs that can't drown include the undead, underwater mobs like squid, and iron golems.

See also: Underwater Breathing.

E–F

ELDER GUARDIANS

Elder guardians are a hostile and rare aquatic mob found only at ocean monuments. They are stronger and larger than their more common counterpart, the guardians, and are a type of boss mob. Only three spawn with each monument, and they will not respawn. You'll usually find them in the wing sections of the monument and in the top room.

Like guardians, elder guardians will attack squid and players, but they don't swim around as much.

You'll find one of the three elder guardians in the top room of the ocean monument.

An elder guardian has three ways to attack you: a ranged laser attack, a spike defensive attack, or a mining fatigue attack. First, if it senses a player that is within a fifty-block range, it will give the status effect Mining Fatigue III for five minutes. This makes it impossible to pickaxe your way through an ocean monument wall, or to break the blocks hiding the gold stash. The attack itself is quite unnerving, as a spectral image of the elder guardian will loom suddenly into your screen with an unearthly screech. When you are close enough (about fourteen blocks) to the elder guardian, and in sight range, it will fire up its lasers. This lasts a few seconds, but when its lasers are fully charged they will deal you a full eight HP of damage (Normal difficulty). Finally, if you attack the elder guardian while its spikes are extended, you'll get another hit of two HP damage.

ELDER GUARDIAN STATS

Type: Hostile

Spawns: Ocean monuments, does not respawn

Health: 80 HP

XP: 10

Damage Hard mode: 12HP

Damage Normal mode: 8HP

Damage Easy mode: 5HP

Damage from spikes: 2 HP

Drops: Raw cod, prismarine crystals, prismarine shards, sponges

Rare drops: Fish other than cod

See also: Guardian, Ocean Monument.

EMPEROR RED SNAPPER

The emperor red snapper is one of Minecraft's tropical fish named for a real tropical fish. In Minecraft's color and pattern scheme, it is a white-red clayfish. The emperor red snapper in real life is a type of snapper and is a fairly large tropical fish (it can grow

Helmet: Aqua Affinity, Level 1 only. Allows you to mine at normal speeds. (Without this, you'll be mining at half speed.)	
Helmet: Respiration, Levels 1–3. Adds fifteen seconds of underwater breathing for each level.	
Boots: Depth Strider, Levels 1–3. Allows you to move faster horizontally underwater.	
Trident: Impaling, Levels 1–5. Inflict extra damage (2.5 HP) to aquatic mobs, except for the undead drowned.	
Trident: Loyalty, Levels 1–3. Makes your trident return to you after you throw it. Higher levels make the trident return more quickly.	
Trident: Riptide, Levels 1–3. Allows you to travel with your trident, as long as you are throwing it while standing in water or in rain.	

up to 4 feet long). It lives in reefs, and when it is young, often lives among the spines of sea urchins for protection.

See also: Red Snapper, Tropical Fish.

ENCHANTMENTS, AQUATIC

There are several enchantments that will particularly help you when you are building or exploring underwater.

Enchanting

To enchant an item with a specific enchantment, you'll need to combine the right enchanted book with the item in an anvil. You can also get random enchantments for the cost of some lapis and XP points using the enchantment table.

See also: Potions, Aquatic.

EXPLORER MAP

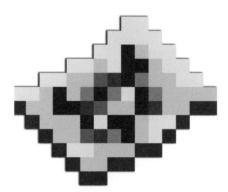

An explorer map is a map that shows you where special structures are. There are three kinds currently: woodland map, which shows the location of a woodland mansion; ocean explorer map, which shows the location of an ocean monument; and buried treasure map, which shows where a loot chest is buried. You must trade with a villager for the first two types of map, and you will need to explore shipwrecks and underwater ruins to find the third.

An explorer map itself shows a 512x512 block area of land, with outlines of land masses surrounded by sea (the orange and brown stripes). The maps show an icon identifying the goal structure and a white marker will show where you are. If you are beyond the area the map covers, the white marker will be placed along one of the map borders. If you are more than 1027 blocks away from the map edge, your marker will be small, and will change to a larger size when you are within 1027 blocks.

To use the map, face north and open the map. The top of the map is north, the direction you are facing. If the white marker showing your position shows you at the left border, you'll need to move right, or east, to reach the treasured area (and vice versa). Similarly, if the white marker is at the top border, you'll move south; if it's at the bottom of the map, you'll move north.

The white marker moves on the map as you move. Once you are on the map's area, the marker has a triangular tip that shows you the direction you are facing. And when you reach the area covered by the map, the map will start filling in with colors.

READING AN EXPLORER MAP

The white player icon at the top left is tiny, showing that you are not near the monument.

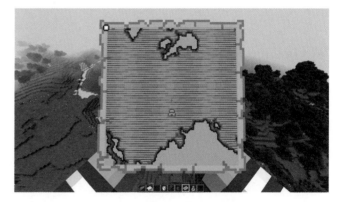

The white player icon is large, showing you are within 1027 blocks from the map's edge.

When you reach the map's edge, the map will start filling in.

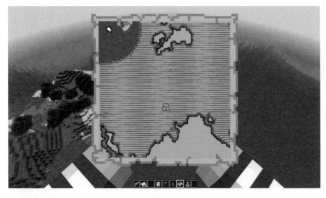

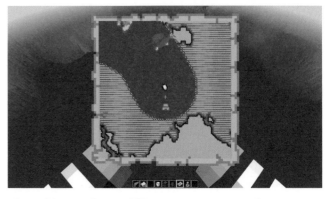

When you enter the map's area, the player icon adds a pointed tip to show the direction you are facing. The map starts filling in with color.

The map continues filling out as you reach your goal.

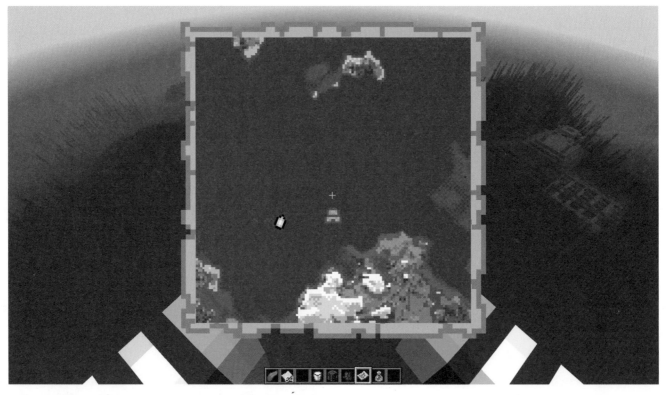

You need to travel around the map to fully flesh it out.

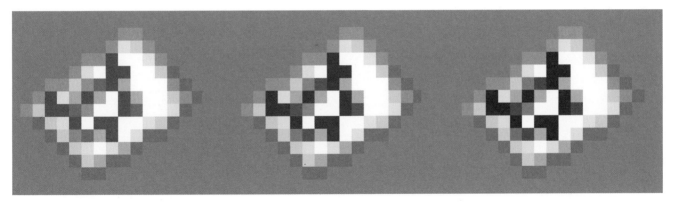

The icons for the three explorer maps use different colors for the writing. From left to right, the ocean map is turquoise, the woodland map is brownish gray, and the buried treasure map is a slightly darker gray.

FISH

Before the 1.13 Update Aquatic, fish were only items. They popped up when you fished, as raw food items, but didn't swim around in the ocean. The 1.13 Update reprogrammed fish as mobs (short for *mobile*). There are four types of fish mobs—cod, salmon, pufferfish, and tropical fish—and each has slightly different behaviors.

However, none will last long out of water; they'll flop around until they suffocate. All can be picked up live with a bucket of water.

See also: Bucket of Fish, Cod, Pufferfish, Salmon, Tropical Fish.

The four types of fish.

FISH STATS

Health: 3 HP

Drops: 1 of the specific fish item, bone meal (rare)

XP: 0

FROZEN OCEAN

The Frozen Ocean Biome has dark, almost purplish surface waters showing between stretches of ice and icebergs. The sea is too cold for kelp or seagrass, although you'll find salmon and squid and drowned. Above water, you may see polar bears, and strays, rather than skeletons, will spawn in these cold temperatures. The Deep Frozen Ocean Biome is very similar to the Frozen Ocean Biome, with two main differences: the ocean surface isn't covered in ice, and the water is deep enough for ocean monuments to generate.

A Deep Frozen Ocean Biome isn't covered in ice.

FROZEN RIVER

The Frozen River Biome is a variant of the River Biome that is only found in a Snowy Tundra Biome. Like a typical River Biome, the riverbed is made of gravel, clay, and sand, but the top level of water, at y=63, is made from ice blocks. A Frozen River can also be generated with a River Biome within or alongside it, so that ice forms at the banks but has water blocks at its center. Seagrass, squid, and salmon are native to this biome.

This Frozen River Biome is intersected by a regular River Biome, which has no ice covering.

G-H

GOATFISH

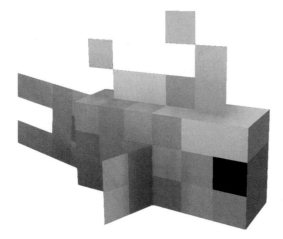

The goatfish is one of Minecraft's twenty-two named tropical fish. In Minecraft's color and pattern scheme, it is a white-yellow spotty. In real life, goatfish are a large family of fish that are part of the mullet family, and not all are tropical. They're known for two barbels (filaments) off of their chin that help them probe the sea floor and for being able to change color. Tropical goatfish live in coral reefs.

See also: Tropical Fish.

GRAVEL

Gravel is the main block that makes up the ocean floor, from Warm Ocean Biomes to Deep Frozen Ocean Biomes. It is one of the few blocks in Minecraft that is affected by gravity: if you place a block midair against another block, the gravel block will drop to place on the nearest block below it. This property makes it very handy for filling in lava pools or deep water. On the flip side, this makes it dangerous if you find yourself directly beneath a column of falling gravel. If you can't step out of the way of the falling gravel, you can suffocate. If falling gravel encounters a non-solid block like a torch, it will break into its item form instead of being placed.

Gravel is also a key ingredient in two other blocks: coarse dirt and concrete powder.

GUARDIAN

The guardian is a hostile aquatic mob that spawns near and inside ocean monuments. They attack squid without mercy and any nearby players. Their main mode of attack is a laser beam shot from their eye: this takes a few moments to power up, giving you time to break their line of sight,

which stops the attack. The guardian has spikes as well, which will inflict damage on a player (two HP) striking it in a melee. Guardians can survive out of water, but will flop about as if they are suffocating. If they're not in attack mode, they'll drift slowly down to the seabed or other solid surface, spikes extended.

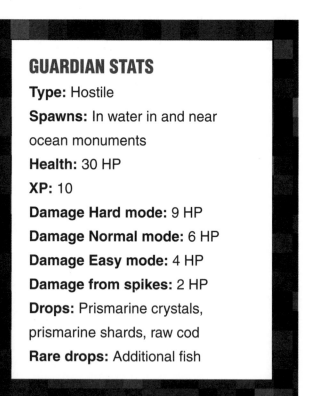

GUARDIAN STATS

Type: Hostile

Spawns: In water in and near ocean monuments

Health: 30 HP

XP: 10

Damage Hard mode: 9 HP

Damage Normal mode: 6 HP

Damage Easy mode: 4 HP

Damage from spikes: 2 HP

Drops: Prismarine crystals, prismarine shards, raw cod

Rare drops: Additional fish

> **The Guardian Eye**
>
> The guardian and elder guardian have a single large eye that will follow a player even if the player is using an Invisibility potion and is unarmored. In programming the model for the guardian, it is the eye that is actually programmed as the head, which is the body part that turns to look at players.

See also: Elder Guardian.

HEART OF THE SEA

The heart of the sea is a rare object found singly in any buried treasure chest. It is a deep blue-green sphere that has a rim separating top from bottom. Currently it has only one use: to craft a conduit, with one heart of the sea surrounded by eight nautilus shells.

See also: Conduit, Nautilus Shell.

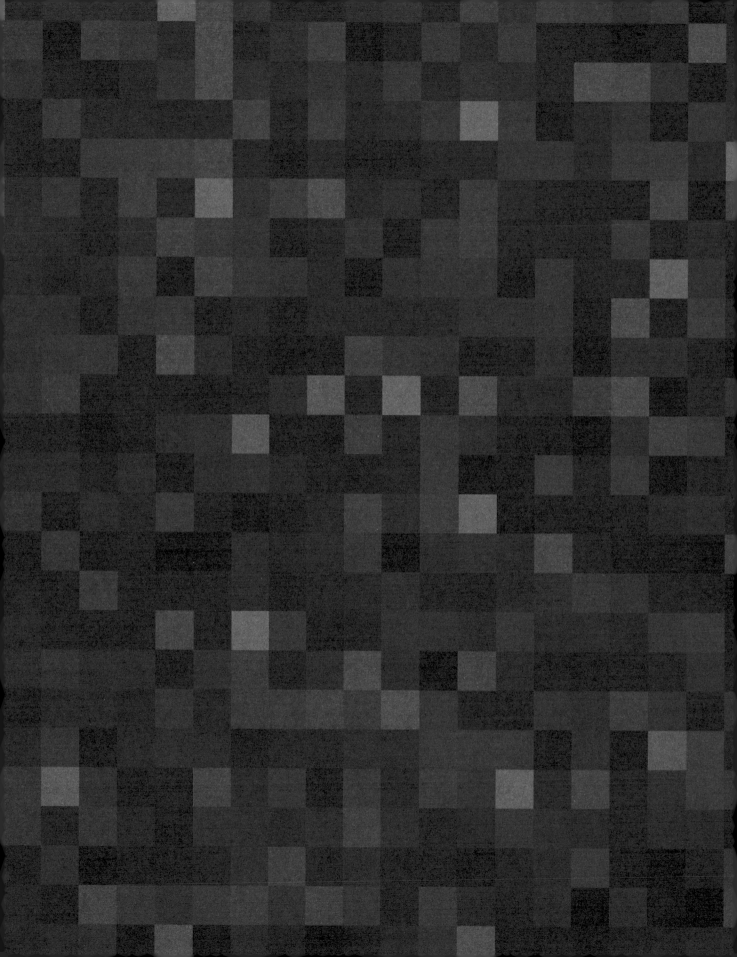

ICE

Ice is one of the naturally generating blocks found at water surface level in Frozen Biomes. It is also found in igloos and icebergs and ice spikes. In Snowy Biomes and Frozen Ocean Biomes, water source blocks will turn into ice as long as the sky is directly above it and one of the sides of the water source blocks is a solid block. Ice will also melt, if any block beside it has a light level greater than eleven from a source other than the sun, like a torch or glowstone.

If you break an ice block that is placed on another block, the ice will turn to a water source. You can only gather ice as a block if you use a Silk Touch pick. One nice feature: ice is a partly transparent block, and mobs other than polar bears can't spawn on it.

See also: Icebergs, Packed Ice, Blue Ice.

Slippery When Ice

All ice block variants—ice, blue ice, and packed ice—have the slippery characteristic. When you walk on them, you'll slide a little. If you throw an item on them, the item will glide a bit. Blue ice is the most slippery, followed by packed ice and then ice. In addition, you can place transparent blocks, like slabs, on top of an ice block, and that block will have the same slippery characteristic. This makes ice a fantastic way to get around speedily in Minecraft.

ICEBERG

Icebergs are a naturally occurring structure found in Frozen and Deep Frozen Ocean Biomes. They appear to be floating in the ocean, with some of their structure below the surface but most above. In size, they can range from small clumps to massive peaks. They're composed mostly of packed ice, often with smaller patches of ice, blue ice, and snow at their tops.

IMPALING

Impaling is an enchantment for the trident weapon. It is similar to Sharpness for a sword, and adds extra damage when you strike (both melee and ranged) an aquatic (and not undead) mob: dolphins, guardians, fish, squid, and turtles. It doesn't work on any other type of mob. There are five levels, and each level adds an extra 2.5 HP of damage.

See also: Trident.

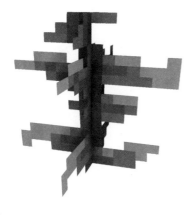

KELP

Kelp is an aquatic plant growing only below the ocean's surface. (It is also the first plant that is animated, its leaves waving back and forth in the water.) You'll find it in Ocean, Lukewarm Ocean, and Cold Ocean Biomes and their Deep variants. It will still grow in Warm and Frozen Oceans if you plant it yourself. It can grow up to the top water block of the sea's surface, but it doesn't need direct access to the sky or any light. It just must be placed in water. In Bedrock Edition, you can bone meal a kelp plant to force it to grow. To harvest a kelp plant, simply break the second block from the ocean floor. All kelp blocks above it will also break, in the same way a chorus plant breaks.

Kelp Magic

Kelp has a unique quality: if it is placed in flowing water, it will turn that water into water source blocks. This means that you can fill up a large area of water by filling just the top layers with water source and flowing blocks, and then place kelp from the bottom layer up to turn all blocks into source blocks.

Kelp will grow from the sea floor all the way up to the top block of ocean water.

LOYALTY

Loyalty is an enchantment that is unique for the trident. It gives a thrown trident the ability to return to the thrower after it hits a block or mob. There are three levels of Loyalty enchantments: the trident returns faster with each higher level. This enchantment isn't compatible with the Riptide enchantment.

See also: Trident, Riptide.

LUKEWARM OCEAN

The Lukewarm Ocean Biome and Deep Lukewarm Ocean Biome have light teal surface waters, only slightly darker than the Warm Ocean Biome. Unlike most of the ocean floor, the seabed here is mostly sand, although you may find a little clay, dirt, or gravel. Kelp and seagrass grow here.

You can find kelp, seagrass, ruins, and shipwrecks here, and underwater ruins here are made mostly of

sandstone. Mobs that spawn underwater in the Lukewarm Ocean Biomes are cod, dolphins, drowned, pufferfish, squid, and tropical fish. The Deep Lukewarm Ocean is twice as deep as the Lukewarm Ocean, which allows ocean monuments to generate here, along with their protectors, the guardians and elder guardians.

MAGMA BLOCK

Magma blocks are found in the Overworld aquatic zones, in underwater ruins, and at the bottom of ravines. They are Minecraft's counterpart to real-life magma, which is a molten rock found underground,

and which becomes lava if it comes to Earth's surface. In Minecraft, although magma doesn't flow, you will find it near lava. Magma blocks are also damaging: entities standing on them will get one HP of damage every tick (there are twenty ticks per second). However, players can Shift (sneak) to avoid this damage. Magma blocks give off a light level of three.

Underwater, a magma block placed under water source blocks (as opposed to flowing water) will create a bubble column. The magma-activated bubble column acts as a whirlpool, pulling entities in the column (including players in boats) down to the magma block.

TIP: Carry a magma block with you underwater so you can place it, and then sneak on it to breathe.

See also: Bubble Columns.

MOORISH IDOL

The Moorish idol is one of Minecraft's tropical fish named for a real-life fish. In Minecraft's color and pattern scheme, it is a white-gray glitter. In real life it is a species of tropical fish with striking bands of white, black, and yellow.

See also: Tropical Fish.

MUSHROOM FIELD SHORE

The Mushroom Field Shore Biome is the one variant of the extremely rare Mushroom Fields Biome. This biome is made of the water, mycelium blocks, sand, clay, and dirt that edge a Mushroom Field, either at an ocean's edge or at the banks of a river that runs through the Mushroom Fields Biome.

NAUTILUS SHELL

The nautilus shell is a Minecraft item used to craft, along with heart of the sea, a conduit. Its real-life counterpart is the shell of the nautilus, an ocean-dwelling, snail-like creature. However, Minecraft doesn't have the animal itself, just its shell. You can get nautilus shells as treasures from fish or as drops from drowned. If a drowned is holding a nautilus shell in their off-hand, it will always be dropped when you kill the drowned.

OBSIDIAN

Underwater, you can find the obsidian block generated along with magma at the bottoms of many underwater ravines. You will also find this wherever a flowing water block meets a lava source block, underwater or over. (Non-aquatic sources of obsidian include generated Nether portals, in Nether fortress chests, in the End, and in woodland mansions.) It is one of the strongest blocks in Minecraft, able to resist explosions, and is used to create beacons, enchantment tables, Ender chests, and Nether portals.

OCEAN

The Ocean Biome is one of the most commonly found of the ocean biomes,

and has surface waters that are a middling blue, lighter than Cold Ocean but darker than Lukewarm. Its floor is made of gravel primarily, along with some patches of clay, dirt, and sand usually near coastlines. You'll find kelp, seagrass, stone ruins, and shipwrecks in ocean biomes. Mobs that spawn underwater in the Lukewarm Ocean Biomes are cod, dolphins, drowned, and squid. The Deep Ocean variant allows for the generation of ocean monuments, complete with elder guardians and guardians.

OCEAN EXPLORER MAP

Ocean explorer maps are a type of explorer map that show you the location of an ocean monument. You can

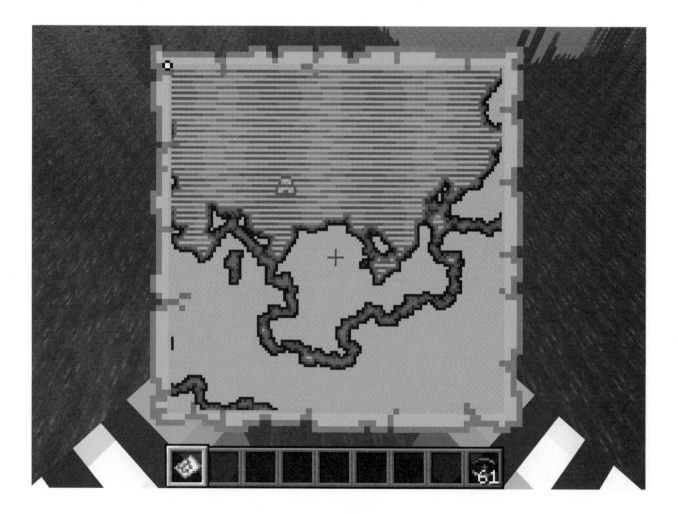

get them only from cartographer villagers (who wear white, like librarians). The cartographer will trade you the map for a compass and somewhere between twelve and twenty emeralds. The map may not show the monument nearest to the cartographer's village, so you may have to travel some distance to find it.

See also: Explorer Map.

OCEAN FLOOR

The ocean floor in Minecraft is made from blocks of gravel or sand, with patches of clay and dirt. In Deep Ocean Biomes, it reaches y=32 and below, and the floors of ravines may reach as low as y=11. In regular ocean biomes, the floor levels at about y=45. However, despite these average levels, the ocean floor rises and dips in shallow or steep valleys, rising at coastlines sharply and in mid-ocean to create islands large

and small. Cold ocean floors (normal through Frozen) are made almost entirely of gravel, along with exposed stones and ores along hills and inclines. Warm ocean floors (Warm and Lukewarm) have a sandy bottom. Dirt and clay are usually found at higher altitudes and at coastlines.

See also: Biomes, Aquatic.

OCEAN MONUMENT

The ocean monument is one of Minecraft's largest generated building structures and is found only in Deep variants of ocean biomes. The rare structure is 58x58 blocks square and twenty-six blocks high and built from prismarine, prismarine bricks, dark prismarine, and sea lanterns.

To help you find an ocean monument, you can trade with a cartographer villager for an ocean explorer map, which will show you the location of one ocean monument.

Each ocean monument has a pillared entryway and two large wings that run the length of the monument. The two wings are connected to each other by a long hallway at the back of the monument. One of the wings is fairly open and contains one of the three elder guardians that spawn with the monument. The second wing has an interior room housing a second elder guardian. The main central building, between the two wings, has a top room that houses the final elder guardians. The other rooms of the

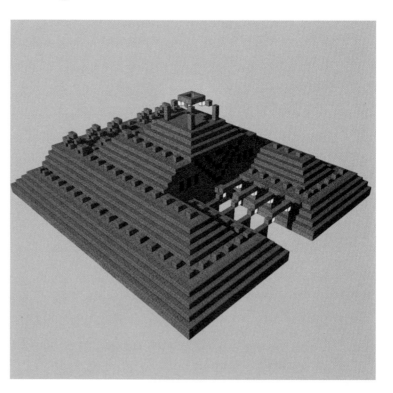

main building are randomly generated with at least six rooms connected in different manners appropriate for swimming inhabitants. A treasure room is always found near the center, with a dark prismarine structure hiding blocks of gold. And there's often a smaller room, usually nearer the top of the building, that houses several sponges you can use to soak up water blocks.

In addition to the three elder guardians, guardian mobs also spawn in and around the ocean monument—it's in fact the only place in the Overworld where they can spawn.

ORNATE BUTTERFLYFISH

The ornate butterflyfish (in BE, ornate butterfly) is one of Minecraft's tropical fish named for a real-life fish. In Minecraft's color and pattern scheme, it is a white-orange clayfish. In real

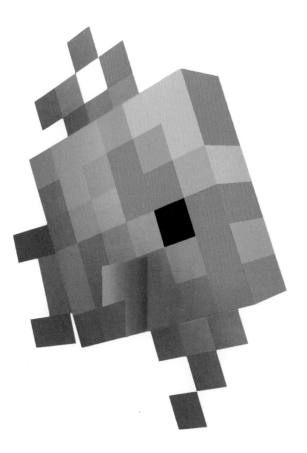

life, this fish is a species found in the butterflyfish family with striking and unusual coloring and patterning: orange stripes and black stripes over a background of blues, greens, lilacs, or white.

See also: Butterflyfish, Tropical Fish.

PACKED ICE

Packed ice is one of three types of ice block generated naturally in the Minecraft world. You'll find it in icebergs in Frozen Ocean Biomes, in the Ice Spikes Biome, in villages in the Snowy Tundra Biomes, and as windows in igloos. You can only harvest packed ice with a Silk Touch pickaxe, but you can craft nine ice into a block of packed ice. It does not melt if light sources are near it, and it is a bit more slippery than regular ice. As a solid block, mobs can spawn on packed ice.

See also: Ice, Blue Ice.

Packed Ice? Really?

Is it at all realistic that Minecraft has different types of ice, with some more condensed than others? A little. In the real world, scientists have so far found (or predicted) about eighteen types of ice that differ in their crystalline shape. These differ from each other in the ways that the molecules of water join with each other into crystals, and this structure changes depending on factors like temperature and pressure. These types of ice are numbered with Roman numerals, from Ice I to Ice II to Ice III and up. On the other hand, pretty much all of the ice on Earth is Ice I. There's no specially slippery blue ice for us to run super fast on.

PARROTFISH

The parrotfish is one of Minecraft's tropical fish named for a real-life fish. In Minecraft's color and pattern scheme, it is a teal-rose dasher. In real life, parrotfish are a family of brightly colored tropical fish known for being able to change sex and coloration throughout their lives. Some parrotfish species are also known for wrapping themselves in a cocoon to help them sleep safely at night. They are named for the shape of their mouth, which looks like the beak of a parrot.

See also: Yellowtail Parrotfish, Tropical Fish.

POTION OF THE TURTLE MASTER

The potion of the Turtle Master is currently the only potion that gives you both a buff (helpful effect) and a debuff (negative effect): Slowness and Resistance. The Resistance effect reduces the amount of damage you can take by 20 percent per level. The Slowness effect slows your walking speed by 15 percent per level.

To brew the potion of the Turtle Master, brew an Awkward potion with a turtle shell. This will give you Slowness IV and Resistance III for twenty seconds. You can then brew this potion with a redstone dust to extend the effect's length to forty seconds. Or, brew the initial potion with one glowstone dust to increase the effects to Slowness VI and Resistance IV.

POTIONS, AQUATIC

There are two potions that will help you manage an underwater trip or existence.

Potion of Water Breathing: This potion allows you to breathe underwater for three minutes (eight minutes for the extended potion) and makes the underwater environment a bit brighter. You make it with a pufferfish brewed with Awkward potion. For the extended potion effects, brew the finished potion again with one redstone dust.

Potion of Night Vision: The potion of Night Vision gives your environment a light level of fifteen, everywhere. Brew it from Awkward potion and a golden carrot for three minutes of light. For eight minutes of light, brew your potion again with one redstone dust.

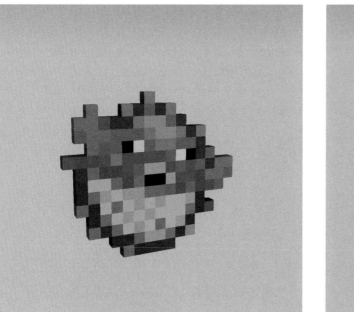

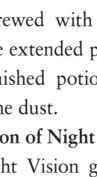

Brewing a Batch

To brew potions, you'll need a brewing stand, blaze powder, Nether wart, water bottles, and the special ingredients that make up a particular potion, like a magma cream for a potion of Fire Resistance. The brewing stand will make up to three potions at a time, and take blaze powder as energy. You first brew an Awkward potion using Nether wart, then brew the Awkward potion with your potion's special ingredients.

PRISMARINE

Prismarine is a truly aquatic block found only underwater as part of the rare ocean monuments and in underwater ruins. It is unique because it is a decorative block that has an animated texture, with veins changing slowly from turquoise to purple and back. Prismarine is also one of the four blocks that can be used to build the activation frame for a conduit. Prismarine is also craftable into prismarine slabs, stairs, and walls, and you can craft a prismarine block itself from four prismarine shards.

Shimmerock?

Jeb Bergensten, lead developer and chief creative officer at Mojang, tweeted for help in naming this aquatic block. Suggestions included shimmerock, shale, seashale, shimmershale, neptone, and flowstone. Ultimately, the name coined by a Reddit user, u/AjaxGb, prismarine—a mashup of prism and marine—was chosen.

See also: Prismarine Bricks, Dark Prismarine, Prismarine Shards.

PRISMARINE BRICK

Prismarine bricks are a decorative block, a variety of prismarine, used to create ocean monuments. This is the only place you will find them naturally, although you can craft them from shards. Both prismarine bricks and dark prismarine have patterns that are reminiscent of tiles rather than bricks, which would be appropriate for their watery use.

See also: Prismarine, Prismarine Shards.

PRISMARINE CRYSTAL

Prismarine crystals are items dropped often by guardians or elder guardians when killed. They are also dropped when you break a sea lantern without using a Silk Touch pick, and you can find them sometimes in buried treasure. You can use prismarine crystals to create sea lanterns.

PRISMARINE SHARDS

Prismarine shards are an item dropped only by guardians or elder guardians when they are killed. *Shard* is a word that refers to a broken, sharp piece of a hard material like glass or rock, so presumably the guardians have been

crunching up prismarine blocks in their spare time! You can use prismarine shards to craft the three varieties of prismarine block and sea lanterns, although you will also need prismarine crystals to create the lanterns.

PUFFERFISH

The pufferfish is one of the four main kinds of fish in Minecraft. You will find them in the warmer ocean biomes: Lukewarm, Deep Lukewarm, and Warm Oceans, often swimming alone, unlike the other fish.

In real life, pufferfish are also called blowfish, known for being highly poisonous and for inflating into a round, inedible shape. Their Minecraft counterparts are the same: they'll blow up to twice their size and give a Poison effect when they are in danger, such as when you or another mob swims too close or when they are damaged. (They will also puff up if you put an armor stand near them.) Skeletons will fight the pufferfish back!

You can get pufferfish from fishing and by catching them live with a water bucket. Pufferfish are also occasionally dropped by guardians and elder guardians when they are killed. Like salmon, pufferfish can swim up a stream of water flowing down.

You can eat a pufferfish, although this will give you three debuffs, or harmful status effects: Hunger III, Nausea II, and Poison IV. You will be hurting for a full minute. The damage you'll get is more than any hunger restored, so don't be right-clicking with a pufferfish in your hand. On the plus side, you can use a pufferfish to tame an ocelot and breed cats, and to brew the very aquatically handy potion of Water Breathing.

The three stages of pufferfish inflation, from top (normal) to bottom (fully inflated).

Fugu About It

Some pufferfish species, like porcupinefish, are seen as a delicacy in Japan and eaten raw. This dish, called *fugu*, is one of the most dangerous foods in the world: the tetrodotoxin poison from a single fish is enough to kill thirty people. Fugu can only be prepared by qualified chefs with years of training who can extract the pufferfish flesh without including the deadly poison in its liver, eyes, skin, and other organs.

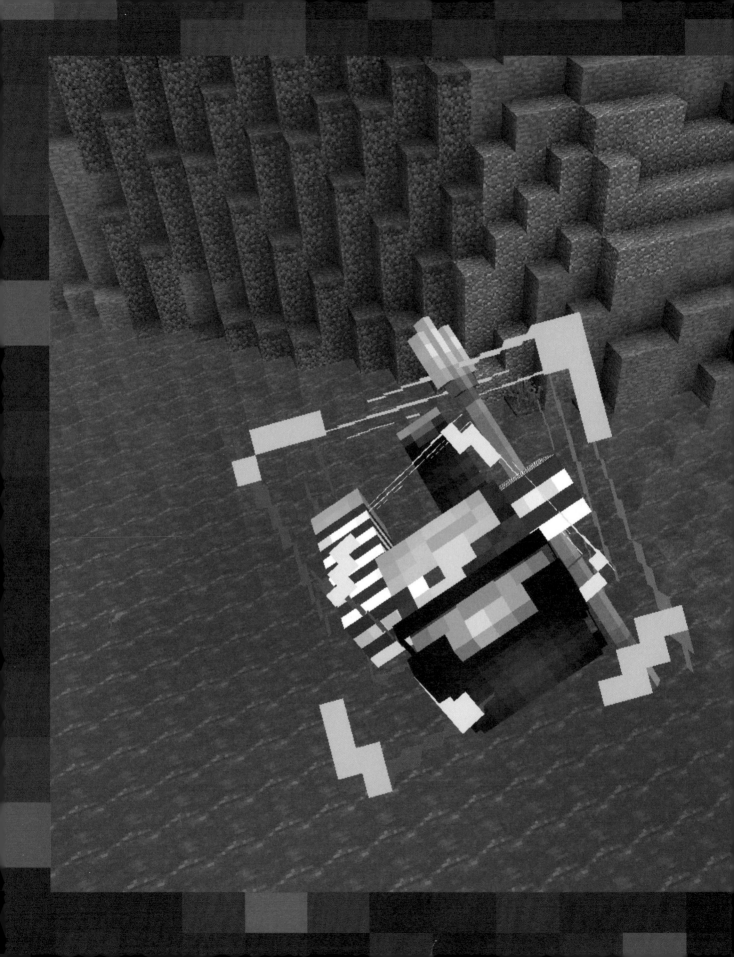

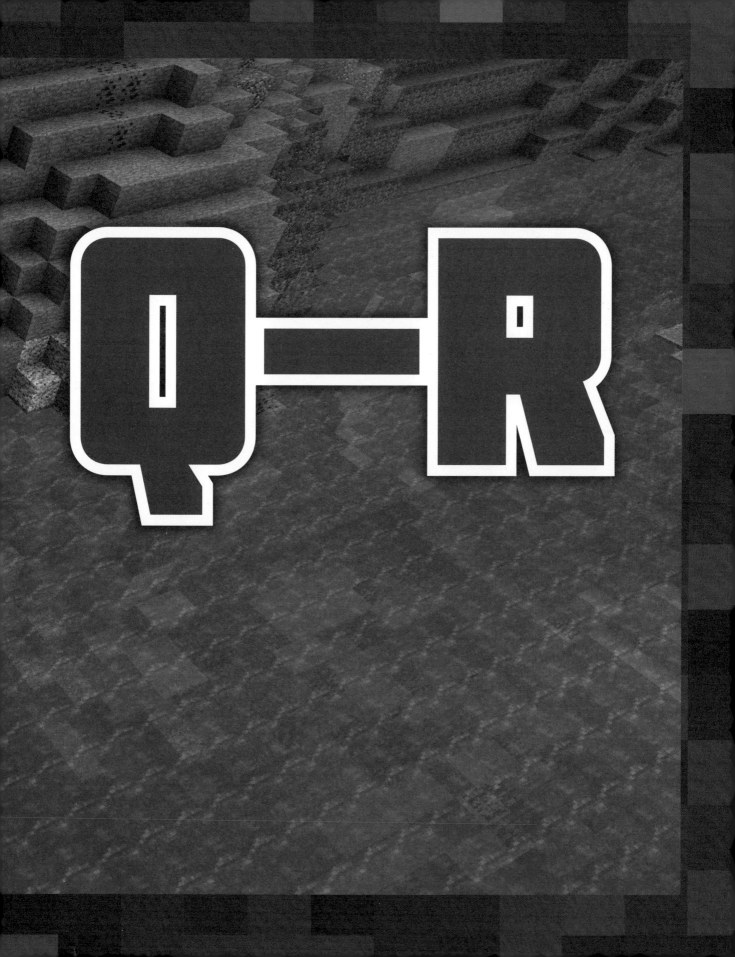

QUEEN ANGELFISH

The queen angelfish (in BE, queen angel fish) is one of Minecraft's twenty-two named tropical fish. In Minecraft's color and pattern scheme, it is a lime-sky brinely. It's named for the real-life queen angelfish, which is a blue and yellow tropical fish that lives near reefs and eats sponges and corals. The angelfish gets its name from a crown-like ring on its head.

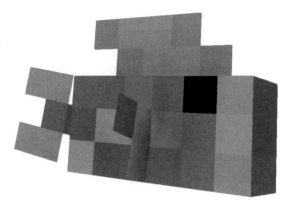

RED CICHLID

Another of Minecraft's named tropical fish, the red cichlid is a red-white betty in the game's color and pattern schemes. In real life, there are many red-colored cichlids, some striped

and some not, including the Dragon Blood Peacock Cichlid, the Red Jewel Cichlid, and the Red Zebra African Mbuna Cichlid. They are part of a large family of cichlids.

See also: Cichlid, Tropical Fish.

RED-LIPPED BLENNY

The red-lipped blenny is one of Minecraft's twenty-two tropical fish that are named for a real-life fish. In Minecraft's color and pattern scheme, it is a gray-red snooper. The real-life redlip blenny (also known as a horseface blenny) is a member of the blennioids, six families of blenny fish

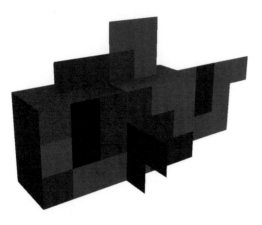

that typically have blunt heads and rounded tail fins. The redlip blenny (named for its reddish lips) is colored brown and lives in shallow coral reefs and is very territorial.

See also: Tropical Fish.

RED SNAPPER

Of Minecraft's twenty-two named tropical fish, the red snapper is likely one of the most familiar, as in real life

it is a popular food fish that lives in reefs in the Gulf of Mexico. In the game's color and pattern scheme, it is a red-white blockfish.

See also: Emperor Red Snapper, Tropical Fish.

RESOURCE CHEAT SHEET

If you're playing a game of bingo in Minecraft or playing an aquatic survival challenge, here's an alphabetical cheat sheet of all ocean resources, including blocks and items and where you can find them! The list doesn't include common ocean floor blocks (clay, dirt, sand, and gravel), mining resources found in caves and below the sea floor, or water. Resource locations that spawn a resource only as a chance are in italics.

AQUATIC RESOURCE CHEAT SHEET

Resource	Source	
Bamboo	*Shipwreck supply chest*	
Birch wood (stripped, planks, fences, stairs, trapdoors, doors)	*Shipwreck*	
Book	*Shipwreck map chests*	
Book and quill	*Buried treasure (BE)*	
Bottles o' Enchanting	*Buried treasure (BE), shipwreck treasure chest*	
Bricks	*Underwater ruins*	
Buried treasure map	*Shipwreck map chests, underwater ruins chest*	
Cake	*Buried treasure (BE)*	
Carrot	*Shipwreck supply chest*	
Chainmail	*Buried treasure (BE)*	
Chest	*Buried treasure, shipwrecks, underwater ruins*	
Clock	*Shipwreck map chests*	

Coal	Shipwreck supply chest	
Cobblestone (regular and mossy)	Underwater ruins	
Cod	Lukewarm Ocean, Ocean, and Cold Ocean Biomes (mob); drop from cod, dolphins, guardians, elder guardians, polar bears (raw); buried treasure (cooked)	
Compass	Shipwreck map chests	
Coral, coral blocks, coral fans	Coral reefs in Warm Ocean Biomes	
Dark oak wood (logs, stripped, planks, fences, stairs, trapdoors, doors)	Shipwreck	
Dark oak planks	Underwater ruins	
Dark prismarine	Ocean monument	
Diamonds	Buried treasure, shipwreck treasure chest	
Dolphins	Any ocean biome except Frozen Ocean	
Emeralds	Buried treasure, shipwreck treasure chest	
Feather	Shipwreck map chests	
Fishing rod	Underwater ruins chest	

Gold	Buried treasure, ocean monument, shipwreck treasure chest	
Granite, polished	Underwater ruins	
Gunpowder	Shipwreck supply chest	
Heart of the sea	Buried treasure	
Ice (normal, blue, packed)	Frozen Ocean Biomes, icebergs	
Ink sac (black dye)	Drop from squid	
Iron	Buried treasure, shipwreck treasure chest	
Iron swords	Buried treasure	
Jungle wood (stripped, planks, fences, stairs, trapdoors, doors)	Shipwreck	
Kelp	Lukewarm Ocean, Ocean, Cold Ocean Biomes	
Lapis lazuli	Shipwreck treasure chest	
Leads	Buried treasure (BE)	
Leather armor	Buried treasure, shipwreck supply chest	
Light blue terra-cotta	Underwater ruins	

Magma blocks	Floor of deep underwater ravines, *underwater ruins*	
Map, empty	*Shipwreck map chests*	
Music discs	*Buried treasure (BE)*	
Name tags	*Buried treasure (BE)*	
Nautilus shell	*Drop from drowned*	
Oak (logs, stripped, planks, fences, stairs, trapdoors, doors)	*Shipwreck*	
Obsidian	Floor of deep underwater ravines near magma blocks, *underwater ruins*	
Paper	*Shipwreck supply chest, shipwreck map chests*	
Potato (regular and poison)	*Shipwreck supply chest*	
Potion of Regeneration	*Buried treasure (BE)*	
Potion of Water Breathing	*Buried treasure (BE)*	
Prismarine	Ocean monuments, *underwater ruins*	
Prismarine bricks	Ocean monuments	

Prismarine crystals	*Buried treasure, drop from guardians, elder guardians, sea lanterns*	
Prismarine shards	*Drop from guardians, elder guardians*	
Pufferfish	Lukewarm and Warm Ocean Biomes	
Pumpkin	*Shipwreck supply chest*	
Purple glazed terra-cotta	*Underwater ruins*	
Rotten flesh	*Drop from drowned, shipwreck supply chest*	
Salmon	Cold and Frozen Ocean Biomes (mob), *buried treasure* (cooked)	
Sandstone (cut, chiseled, regular, stairs)	*Underwater ruins*	
Scute	Drop from baby turtle maturing	
Seagrass	All ocean biomes except Frozen Oceans	
Sea lanterns	*Underwater ruins*	
Sea pickles	Lukewarm and Warm Ocean Biomes	
Snow	Frozen Ocean Biomes, icebergs	

Sponge	*Ocean monuments,* drop from elder guardian	
Spruce wood (logs, stripped, planks, fences, stairs, trapdoors, doors)	*Shipwreck*	
Spruce planks	*Underwater ruins*	
Stone bricks (regular, chiseled, cracked, mossy, stairs)	*Underwater ruins*	
Suspicious stew	*Shipwreck supply chest*	
TNT	*Buried treasure, shipwreck supply chest*	
Trident	*Drop from drowned*	
Tropical fish	Warm Ocean Biomes	
Turtle	Beaches	
Turtle eggs	Placed by turtles bred with seagrass	
Turtle shells	Crafted from scutes	
Wheat	*Shipwreck supply chest*	

RIPTIDE

Riptide is one of the four unique enchantments for the trident. It turns the trident from a weapon into a form of transportation, in which you hurtle into the sky, spinning as you go. To use it, you must be in some form of contact with water. It must be raining or you must be standing in water or underwater. Then you can throw your Riptide-enchanted trident to move with it with a charged spinning effect. You can inflict a mob with ranged attack damage, if you and your trident hit it. With each successive level of Riptide (up to level III), you can travel farther. You can't enchant a Riptide trident with Loyalty or Channeling, but you can enchant it with Impaling.

See also: Trident, Loyalty, Channeling, Impaling.

RIVER

The River Biome is a narrow long biome that is often a border between two other biomes. These rivers carve out a path in the land's surface and are filled with water source blocks. The riverbed is composed of gravel, sand, and clay, and lies typically around y=56. The water level is the same as sea level, at y=63. The width of the river itself ranges between a few blocks wide to fifteen or more blocks wide, but the biome can include the banks of the river. The River Biome's flora and fauna include seagrass, sugar cane, squid, and salmon.

SALMON

Salmon are one of the four types of fish in Minecraft. They spawn in the Cold and Frozen Ocean Biomes as well as River and Frozen River Biomes. You'll often find them swimming in schools with other salmon. You can fish for salmon and catch them live with a water bucket. Raw salmon is also a possible drop when you kill guardians or polar bears, and cooked salmon can be found in buried treasure chests. As with other fish, you can use salmon to tame ocelots, lure annoying cats from beds and chests, and breed cats. In the Bedrock Edition, salmon can be small, normal, or large. You can feed a dolphin salmon, too, and it will lead you to a loot chest in a shipwreck or underwater ruins!

See also: Fish.

SAND

Sand is one of the four main blocks that make up the ocean floor as well as beaches and coastlines. (Red sand, a variant, is only found in badlands biomes.) Sand is one of the few blocks, like gravel, that is affected by gravity. This property means it falls if it is placed without a block beneath it, and breaks if it falls on a non-solid block like a torch. Sand is used to craft concrete powder, sandstone, and TNT, and smelted to make glass. Cactus must be, and sugar cane can be, grown on sand.

SCUTE

Scutes are bony plates on turtle shells, and baby turtles crop one scute when they mature into adult turtles. You can use the bright green scute item to craft turtle shells, a type of helmet. You can also brew a scute with Awkward potion to create potion of the Turtle Master.

See also: Turtle Shell, Potion of the Turtle Master.

SEA LANTERN

Sea lanterns are one of the light-emitting blocks in Minecraft, giving out light at a level of fifteen, the brightest light possible. You can find them naturally generated only as part of ocean monuments and underwater ruins. It is one of the few blocks that can be used to activate a conduit.

Light Fantastic

Minecraft's sixteen possible light levels go from zero to fifteen. Blocks are given a brightness level according to the light level. Daylight gives blocks a light level of fifteen. A light source gives out light at a level specific to that source. Magma blocks give a light level of three, a single sea pickle has a level of six, a torch gives a light level of fourteen, and glowstone and sea lanterns give out light at a level of fifteen. Light from light sources other than the sun decrease by one level for each block away from the source. That means a stone block next to a sea lantern will start at light level fourteen; the sea lantern light on a block five blocks away will be level ten.

To harvest a sea lantern, you must break it with a pick enchanted with Silk Touch. Otherwise, it will drop a few prismarine crystals, but not enough to craft a replacement sea lantern block. To craft a sea lantern block, you need four prismarine shards and five prismarine crystals.

SEA PICKLE

Although sea pickles in real life are animals, in Minecraft the sea pickle behaves very similarly to a plant. It resembles an upright, green pickle, and is found in Lukewarm and Warm Ocean Biomes on the ocean floor or on coral blocks. You can place up to four sea pickles on the same block. If you use bone meal on a sea pickle, you will not only grow more pickles (again, up to four) on the same block, but there's also a chance the pickles will expand to adjacent live coral blocks. A solitary sea pickle generates a light level of 6, two generate 9, three generate 12, and four generate 15 light levels.

In real life, sea pickles are also known as pyrosomes, tubular colonies

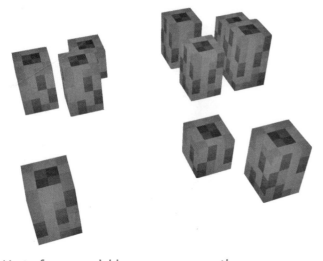

Up to four sea pickles can spawn on the same block. The more sea pickles, the brighter they are.

of thousands of tiny ocean animals called zooids. The colonies float around in the ocean, although they can slowly move themselves. They are also known for being luminescent, shining a pale greenish blue light underwater.

SEAGRASS

Seagrass is a plant that grows on the sea floor in all ocean biomes but the Frozen Ocean. You can also find it in rivers, swamps, and waterlogged caves. Like kelp, it's one of the few animated plant blocks in Minecraft.

Seagrass comes in two sizes: one block high and two blocks high. You can grow seagrass by using bone meal on any solid block underwater, but you can gather it only with shears. Bone meal will also grow a one-block-tall seagrass into a two-block-tall seagrass.

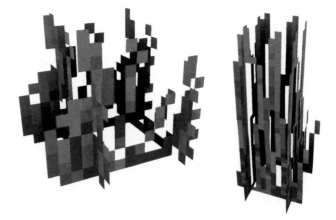

Seagrass can be one or two blocks high.

You can lure and breed turtles with seagrass, and turtles will sometimes drop seagrass when they are killed.

SHIPWRECKS

Long, long ago in Minecraft, apparently, there were pirates! Given what they've left behind for us to find, these pirates were vegetarians that traveled in three-masted ships and were lousy navigators and sailors. We know this because they buried treasure, left many treasure maps with villagers, and wrecked every single ship. All we have left now are the loot chests, the maps, and the shipwrecks. If you study the supplies left in their ships' chests, you can see other clues to their lives and interests. In fact, the height of the passageway to the captain's cabin seems to indicate that at least the captains were shorter than a

villager or player. You'll want to carry an axe with you when you explore to get rid of the slab at the top of that doorway.

Game-wise, shipwrecks are a structure generated with Minecraft's terrain, and you can find them typically submerged in oceans, as well as occasionally on coastlines and sometimes even in or beside rivers. The ships are made entirely of wood, and in most cases are missing chunks of their structure, like the bow or stern or masts. They may be sunk on their side or even upside down. They are typically constructed with the planks and logs of two different types of wood, except for acacia planks and logs. There are actually twenty different shipwreck models in various states of decay that can be generated with different combinations of wood.

Most important, however, are the one to three loot chests contained within a ship. In the captain's cabin, at the back of the ship off the main (top) deck, you'll find the treasure chest.

Belowdeck there are two more chests. In the back room over the rudder, you'll find the map chest. At the front or bow, you'll find another room, the forecastle, with a supply chest. Not all shipwrecks have all three chests, though: if a ship is missing a chest's location, it's missing that chest.

You'll get a random assortment of possible goodies in the three types of chests.

Treasure chest: bottles o' enchanting, diamonds, emeralds, gold ingots and nuggets, lapis lazuli, iron ingots and nuggets.

Map chest: Books, buried treasure map, clocks, compasses, empty maps, feathers, paper.

Supply chest: Bamboo, carrots, coal, gunpowder, leather armor, rotten flesh, paper, potatoes, pumpkin, suspicious stew, TNT, wheat.

SNOW

Snow blocks are one of the blocks naturally generated as part of Frozen

to gather four snowballs from it. A Silk Touch pick will let you gather the block itself.

Snow blocks are used in the igloo structures of Minecraft. You can also craft snow golems from two blocks of snow and a carved pumpkin (or Jack o' Lantern).

Ocean Biomes, as part of icebergs (usually the tips), as well as in other snowy biomes. Snow is an easily broken block, but you must use a shovel

SNOWY BEACH

You'll find the rare Snowy Beach Biome whenever a snowy land biome

meets the ocean. Although the beach is sand, it is usually covered in layers of snow, and ocean water at its edge turns to ice. It is too cold for turtles to spawn here. As with other coastlines, pirates of the past have buried treasure and sunk their ships here.

> ## The Snowy Biomes
>
> Snowy Taiga: Land of spruce trees, snow, and wolves. This biome has two variants: Snowy Taiga Hills and rare Snowy Taiga Mountains. The Snowy Tundra Biome is a flat expanse of snow with some trees. This biome also has two variants: Snowy Mountains and the rare Ice Spikes, which is crowded with large spikes of packed ice.

SPONGE

Sponges are one of the rarest blocks in Minecraft. They can't be crafted; you can only find them in the ocean monument sponge rooms (if they are generated) or as a drop from an elder guardian. Elder guardians don't respawn, and there are only three per monument, so the total number of sponges in a world is limited by the number of ocean monuments found. A sponge room in an ocean monument typically contains around thirty sponges.

Sponges can be wet or dry. If they are wet, you can dry them in a furnace. Once dry, a sponge placed in water can soak up dozens of nearby water source blocks, after which they must be dried again.

In real life, sponges are a group of ancient aquatic animals that survive by attaching to a surface and having water flow through their channels and pores to help collect food and oxygen, and remove waste. They're often shaped like hollow tubes to help the water flow through them. Their makeup includes spongin, a material that makes them soft. Some sponges are grown commercially to sell as bathroom sponges often called "natural sea wool sponges." The soft spongy material these are made of are actually the animal's skeleton.

SQUID

The squid holds the honor of being Minecraft's first aquatic mob. (Fish have been items but only mobs since the Aquatic Update.) It is a passive mob, nearly two blocks high, with eight long arms. As the squid swims, its arms open and close, as if it is moving by jet propulsion, as real-life squid do. As it rolls about in the water, you can see its red open mouth surrounded by teeth on its bottom surface. Squid can spawn in any biome in water at levels from y=46 to sea level, y=63. If you strike them, squid will release a black ink cloud from their bottom mouth as they try to escape, and if you kill them, they will drop ink sacs. At ocean monuments, they are the constant prey of the guardians' laser beams.

> ### Got Squilk?
> When squid were first introduced into Minecraft's Java Edition Beta 1.2, you could milk them. You could just right-click them as you would a cow and get a bucket of white milk. This interesting characteristic was phased out by Beta 1.4.

STONE SHORE

The Stone Shore Biome is a variant of the Beach Biome, and generates only when a Mountain or Wooded Biome meets an Ocean Biome. The shoreline is made only of stone and occasional gravel patches and usually falls steeply into the ocean.

SWAMP

The Swamp Biome is a waterlogged lowland, where shallow water is interspersed with usually flat patches of land. The water is a murky greenish color, often just one block deep at sea level. However, some swamp areas may be lower than sea level, giving deeper pools. The swamp floor is

made of mostly dirt with patches of clay. Seagrass grows in the swampy water and lily pads above it. A unique type of oak tree grows in swamps, both in water and on land. These oaks are broader and wider than typical oak trees, and vines grow from their leaves to the ground. They are only created with the terrain generation, so you cannot grow them from an oak sapling. Other flora and fauna specific to the swamp include blue orchids, sugar cane, mushrooms, fossils, and slimes. Witch huts, along with witches, can also generate in the Swamp Biome. There is a rarer, hillier variant of the Swamp Biome called Swamp Hills; these do not have witch huts or slimes.

SWIMMING

Swimming in Minecraft is much like walking; just press W or your forwards key to move in the direction you are

looking. You can even sprint-swim (as long as your hunger level is above three haunches) by pressing the same sprint button or tapping W (or forwards) twice. Like sprinting on land, this will cause you to lose haunches on your hunger bar faster. To swim down more quickly, press Shift or the sneak button. When you swim, your size changes so that you can fit through one-block-high spaces—so make your hidden underwater base with this in mind!

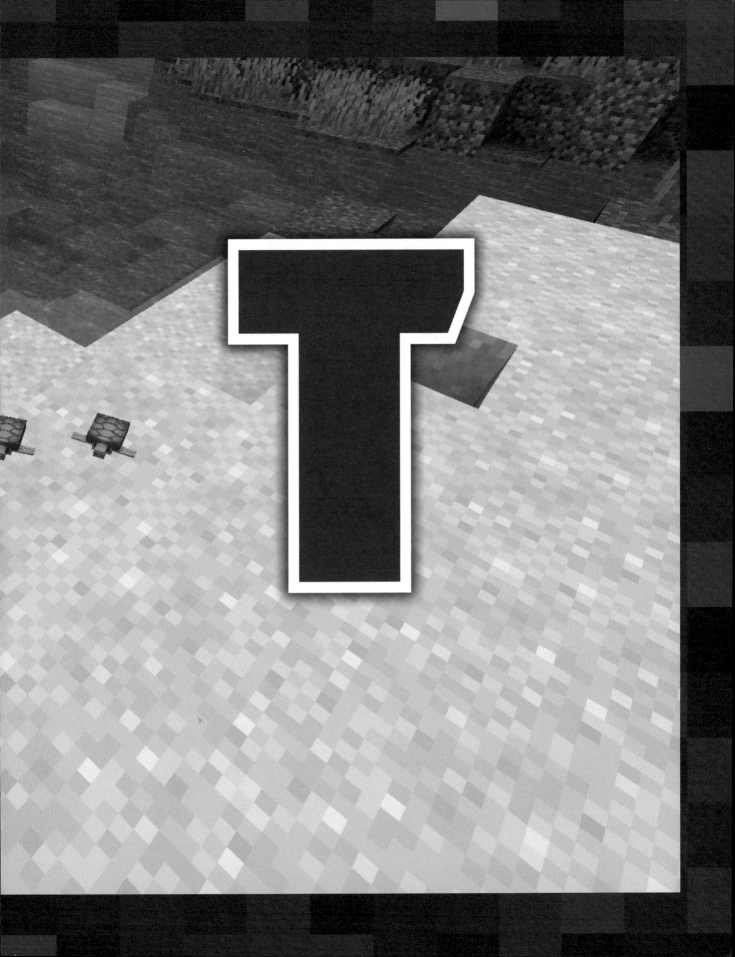

THREADFIN

The threadfin is one of the twenty-two tropical fish that make an appearance in Minecraft. In Minecraft's color and pattern scheme, the threadfin is a white-yellow flopper. In real life, there are several species of threadfin, the largest of which can reach over 6 feet long, and they are a popular food fish. They're known for having long, thin streamers coming from their pectoral (side) fins.

See also: Tropical Fish.

TOMATO CLOWNFISH

The tomato clownfish (called the tomato clown in BE) is one of Minecraft's tropical fish named for a real-life fish. In Minecraft's color and pattern scheme, it is a red-white sunstreak (in BE, red-white kob). It is a member of the clownfish (anemonefish) family known for their symbiotic relationship with sea anemones. This clownfish is an orangey red with a distinctive white bar, outlined with black, beside their eyes.

See also: Anemone, Clownfish, Tropical Fish.

The Beta Edition of the tomato clown/clownfish (top) and the Java Edition (bottom).

TRIDENT

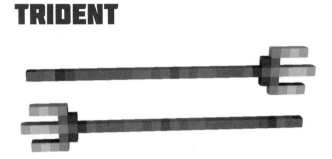

Tridents are long, forked spears used for combat in Minecraft. You can only get them by killing a drowned, which will occasionally drop a trident when killed. This is a more likely drop if you see the drowned actually holding a trident, but less than a fifth of drowned will spawn holding a trident. If they do, watch out. Even though their tridents aren't enchanted, they can throw them infinitely and you cannot pick their thrown tridents up for your own use. Unlike arrows, tridents travel at full speed underwater. If a drowned is holding a trident in their offhand, it will always be dropped when you kill that drowned.

When you are lucky enough to get yourself a trident, you can use it in both melee and ranged attacks, enchant it, and use it for some fancy

maneuvers. In a melee attack, the trident delivers nine HP of damage and thirteen HP of damage with a critical hit. As with a sword, a critical hit is made when you strike as you fall after jumping. In a ranged attack, you will deal eight HP of damage. In a ranged attack, you do need to charge the trident by holding it for a few moments, and as your weapon, you can retrieve it after it hits its target. If you are the unlucky recipient of a trident attack, a shield will block the attack. The enchantments you can use with a trident include Mending, Unbreaking, Impaling, Loyalty, Riptide, and Channeling. Tridents are enchanted

and repaired in the same way as other tools and weapons.

See also: Channeling, Impaling, Loyalty, Riptide.

Trident: Impaling, Levels 1–5. Inflict extra damage (2.5 HP) to aquatic mobs, except for the undead drowned.

Trident: Loyalty, Levels 1–3. Makes your trident return to you after you throw it. Higher levels make the trident return more quickly.

Trident: Riptide, Levels 1–3. Allows you to travel with your trident, as long as you are throwing it while standing in water or in rain.

TRIGGERFISH

The triggerfish is one of Minecraft's tropical fish named for a real-life fish. In Minecraft's color and pattern scheme, it is a gray-white sunstreak. In real life, the triggerfish belongs to a family of tropical fish found typically in coral reefs. They are usually colored and oval shaped, and have strong jaws and teeth for eating shelled animals. They are known for being very territorial and aggressive.

See also: Tropical Fish.

The Melee Milieu

In the land of games, ranged attacks are those that use weapons that fire a projectile over long distances, like crossbows and spears. Melee attacks are close-quarter fights with weapons like axes and swords, that operate at hand-to-hand distance. In real life, melee can also mean actual hand-to-hand combat or a noisy brawl in general.

TROPICAL FISH

Tropical fish are one of the four main types of fish mobs in Minecraft. They're found only in the Warm Ocean Biomes, where they usually travel in small schools of the same type. A tropical fish can be one of twelve models or patterns using up to two different colors from a choice of fifteen colors, which means there are thousands (3,584, to be precise) of possible varieties of tropical fish. However, most (about 90 percent) spawn as one of twenty-two named fish with a specific color and design model. These are named after real-life tropical fish and have colorings similar to their counterparts. Their colors relate to standard Minecraft colors but some are named differently: blue, brown, gray, green, lime, magenta, orange, plum (purple), red, rose (pink), silver (light gray), sky (light blue), teal (cyan), yellow, and white.

The twenty-two named tropical fish are: anemone, black tang, blue tang/blue dory, butterflyfish, cichlid, clownfish, cotton candy betta, dottyback, emperor red snapper, goatfish, Moorish idol, ornate butterflyfish, parrotfish, queen angelfish, red cichlid, red-lipped blenny, red snapper, threadfin, tomato clownfish, triggerfish, yellow tang, and yellowtail parrotfish.

See also: Individual entries for named fish, Fish.

The twelve models of tropical fish, using a white base and gray pattern color.

Betty

Blockfish

Glitter

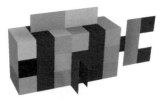

Kob

Snooper

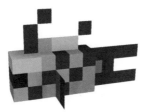

Spotty

Brinely

Clayfish

Stripey

Sunstreak

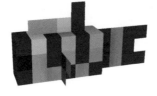

Dasher

Flopper

TURTLE

Turtles are a passive mob and spawn during world generation on sandy beaches, at light level seven or up. They will only spawn on blocks from level y=60 to y=67. They will swim in

water nearby as well as roam a bit on land. Like dolphins, turtles have more complex behavior than most passive mobs: they remember the beach they spawn on as their home beach and return to their home beaches to lay eggs. If you breed two turtles (with seagrass), one of the turtles gets bigger and on its home beach will scrape at the sand and place its turtle eggs (one to four) on a sand block.

Turtles swim in water and roam on land. With thirty HP, they have much higher health than most passive mobs. Most passive mobs have ten HP or lower, and currently only horses can reach as high as thirty HP. Also, unlike most passive mobs, you can't use a lead on them.

Baby turtles may occasionally spawn alongside adult turtles. You can use their favorite food (seagrass) to speed their growth into adults. When they do turn into adults, they drop a single scute: a portion of turtle shell. As with other mobs, you can use their favorite food to lure turtles in the same way you use wheat to lure cows.

In real life, turtles are one of the oldest types of reptiles and a number of turtle species are endangered. In Minecraft, the turtle mob is also in danger: baby turtles are sought out and killed by all types of zombies and skeletons, as well as by ocelots and wolves.

A turtle with an egg (right) has a fatter stomach than a regular turtle.

Baby turtles are tiny and many hostile mobs will attack them.

TURTLE STATS

Type: Passive

Spawns: Sandy beaches

Health: 30 HP

XP: 1–3

Drops: Seagrass, scute (when baby matures)

Rare drops: None

TURTLE EGGS

Turtle eggs are placed on sand blocks by turtles that have been bred. Up to four turtle eggs can be placed at a time on a block, and the eggs change twice, their spots darkening and increasing in number before hatching. Turtle eggs themselves are in danger of being stomped on. The eggs actually lure nearby zombies and their variants, like the drowned, to them; the zombies will stomp on them until they break. Eggs will hatch only at night, and each egg will hatch one tiny turtle. You can pick up eggs by breaking them with a Silk Touch pickaxe.

The three stages of turtle eggs hatching, shown for one through four eggs, the maximum a turtle can lay.

TURTLE SHELL

In Minecraft, turtle shells are helmets made of scutes, the bony plates of shells that baby turtles drop when they mature into adults. Five scutes can craft one turtle shell. These helmets give you the effect of Water Breathing for ten seconds, starting from when you submerge. You can also enchant them with other armor enchantments. Turtle shells have a high durability, more than iron, and give two defense points against damage. Turtle shells are also used in brewing to create the potion of the Turtle Master.

UNDERWATER BUILDING TECHNIQUES

There are a variety of techniques you can use for underwater building. Your top enemies in building underwater are breathing, breaking blocks quickly, and getting rid of water to make air spaces.

Build from a Door

You can start very simply underwater by placing a door that allows you to breathe in its space. Place solid blocks for walls and roofs, and use sand or sponges to soak up water source blocks.

Build from a Tunnel

Dig down at a coastline, and either at the sea floor or above it, build (or dig) a tunnel out to where you want your base to be. At your tunnel exit, create a roof extending out from the exit. Remove air blocks beneath the roof with sand to create an air pocket.

With a sand-mold strategy, build a mold of the internal air space of your building on top of a dirt platform, using sand. Make sure the ocean floor below is flat.

Excavation Site

You can clear out an entire section of ocean by dropping sand (or gravel) into the area you are building. Essentially, you are replacing an entire chunk of ocean from the sea floor to the surface with blocks. The lower you are building, the longer this takes. Once this is done, dig out the interior of your sand chunk and construct your building in this new empty space. Once you're finished building, you'll have to replace any exterior air blocks on the sides and above your building with water blocks, so the more water needed above your build, the more tedious this is.

Sand Molds

You can build a mold of your structure on blocks right above the area where you want your underwater building. You'll want to build above a flat area, because the sand mold will

Break the dirt platform so the sand mold will fall to the ocean floor.

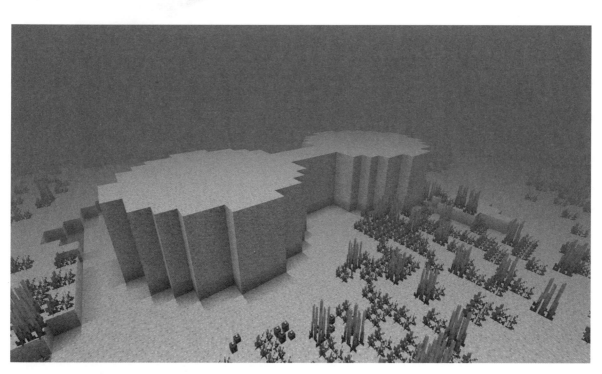

The sand mold below will be exactly the same as above.

Build the walls and ceilings around the sand mold.

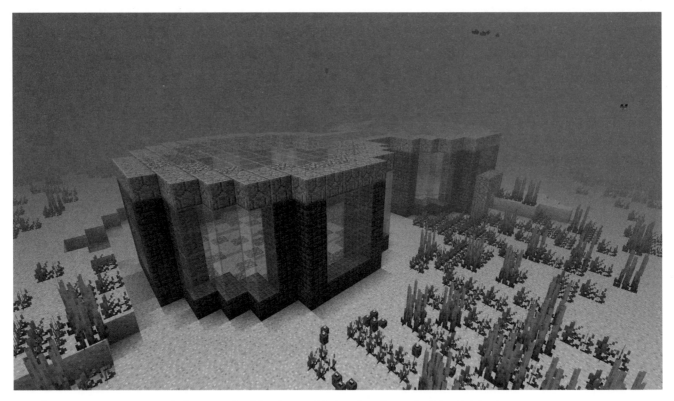

Finally, you can remove all the sand inside the mold, leaving breathable air blocks.

change shape according to the sea levels below. Use easy-to-break blocks as a base. When you finish your mold, break the base blocks so that the sand falls, making the same shape on the sea floor as it had above the ocean surface. Then you can place building blocks around the underwater mold to create its walls and ceiling. Leave a space to enter the mold and then remove the sand.

BUILDING ON WATER

If you are far from shore, the lily pad is your building friend: it's one of the few blocks you can place on water to get you started with placing blocks. You can also place blocks above a tall kelp plant.

See also: Underwater Survival.

UNDERWATER BUILDING TYPES

Minecraft starts you out with a hint of what's possible for underwater buildings with the underwater ruins you can find in all oceans. These look like small homes, temples, and remnants of tiny communities. Besides houses, there are dozens of underwater structures, real and fantasy, that you can build, including aquariums, dolphin habitats and resorts, cities, mermaid habitats, monuments, marine research stations, restaurants, hotels, spas, ravine cliff houses, ravine dwellings, resource farms and factories, secret bases (military, UFO, resistance, superhero), submarines, sunken ships, survival habitats, temples and religious buildings, and turtle rescue and research centers.

UNDERWATER CAVES

Underwater caves are caves found below sea level that are filled with water rather than air. You'll have to explore them while swimming, with good underwater breathing aids. Some underwater caves may have openings directly into the ocean waters or branch out from underwater ravines. Others are simply water-filled caves beneath the ocean floor. If an underwater cave is low enough for its floor to reach y=11, it may feature the same patches of magma block and obsidian that are found in deep underwater ravines.

UNDERWATER RAVINES

Underwater ravines generate in both regular and Deep Ocean biomes. Like their land counterparts, they can be thirty or more blocks deep and a hundred or more blocks long. Unlike them, they are filled with water. Underwater ravines that reach down to y=11 may have sections of their narrow floors turned to obsidian and magma, as if the ocean water here had met lava flowing up from the Earth's crust. The magma blocks create bubble columns that reach to the surface and can pull down mobs that are caught in them, low enough to be damaged or killed by the magma block that is their source.

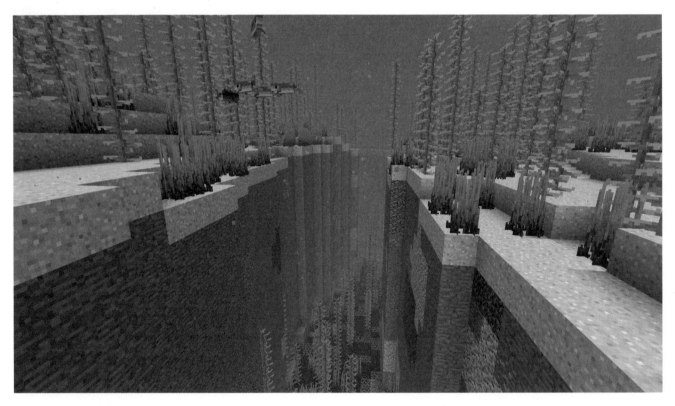

UNDERWATER RUINS

Underwater ruins are relatively small structures that are generated on the ocean floor. If the ocean floor is shallow enough, portions of the ruins may extend above sea level, and some ruins may generate on beaches. These ruins look to be the remnants of small houses or temples. In warm oceans (warm to lukewarm), the ruins are constructed from mostly sandstone and sandstone variations. In colder oceans (normal to frozen), the ruins are made from mostly stone brick and stone brick variations. Other blocks you'll find at ruins include prismarine, gravel, sand, polished granite, bricks,

In oceans with sandy floors, underwater ruins are constructed from sandstone.

Not all underwater ruins are underwater—you can find some on or close to a beach.

planks, and, more rarely, polished diorite, purple-glazed terra-cotta, or light blue terra-cotta.

The ruins often include sea lanterns, magma blocks, and a loot chest that is usually buried beneath a block of sand. If you are looking for these ruins, keep an eye out for squared shapes and lights underwater. Be wary, however, because underwater ruins are spawning locations for the drowned, so you will have some company on your treasure hunts.

The loot you can get from underwater ruins includes buried treasure maps, coal, emeralds, enchanted books, enchanted fishing rods, gold nuggets, gold helmets, golden apples, leather armor, rotten flesh, stone axes, and wheat.

UNDERWATER SURVIVAL

To survive underwater, you need the same things as you do aboveground to survive, plus two important extras: oxygen and normal mining speed.

Food: You can start with drying kelp and punching fish! Once you have a furnace and coal, you won't lack for cooked cod and salmon.

Shelter: You'll need to find an under-the-ocean cave that is not waterlogged, clear out the water from a shipwreck, or build a shelter from scratch.

Sleep: You'll need to find some spiders or mineshafts in caves underwater to get enough string to make wool for a bed.

Armor, weapons, and tools: You can find some armor and weapons in loot chests, but you'll need to start a mine and prevent it from filling with water.

Oxygen: Your ultimate goal will be a series of activated conduits; in the meantime, you can place a door for emergency breathing.

Mining speed: Your mining will be hampered until you can get a helmet enchanted with Aqua Affinity or activate a conduit.

See also: Breathing, Resource Cheat Sheet, Underwater Building Techniques, Project: Make a Water World.

PROJECT: MAKE A WATER WORLD

A water world is a world without land, just ocean. Without any land, you're going to have a tough time getting resources to live on. Your priorities will include building an above-water surface area to live on, and securing food and shelter. You can build up from a structure, like a shipwreck or even kelp, close to the water surface. You also want to find wood (a shipwreck will have plenty) to create a boat and tools. For food, raw fish will have to do to start with, and sitting in a boat will keep your hunger levels from falling.

If you're ready for the real challenge of surviving in a Water World, you have some options. First, you can download a premade map from sharing sites like Project Minecraft. Within Minecraft, there are a few ways to make a Water World.

Use a Built-In Preset World

A preset world is a type of Superflat world where you specify how many flat layers of blocks, and which blocks, make up the Overworld. The default Superflat world has just four layers: one bottom layer of bedrock, two layers of dirt, and a top layer of grass. You can use or configure predefined combinations, called presets, to have more layers of different types of blocks. You could make a Superflat world of diamond block, for example.

1. Start Minecraft. On your launcher start screen, select Singleplayer.

2. On the Select World screen, click Create New World.

3. On the Create New World screen, type in the name for your world and click More World Options.

4. On the Create New World: More World Options screen, click the World Type button to change this to Superflat.

5. Below the World Type: Superflat button, click the Customize button.

6. On the Superflat Customization screen, click the Presets button.

7. The Presets screen lists a number of different preconfigured Superflat options. Select Water World and click the Use Preset button.

8. Back on the Superflat Customization screen, you can see the layers that will
    be created for the world: ninety layers of water on top of sand, dirt, stone,
    and finally one layer of bedrock.

9. Ninety layers of water will make it next to impossible to survive, but you can adjust this. Click the Preset button again, and notice the text box at the top of the screen. This shows the code for specifying the layers of the world. It reads: **minecraft:bedrock,5*minecraft:stone,5*minecraft:dirt,5*mine craft:sand,90*minecraft:water;minecraft:deep_ocean;oceanmonument, biome_1**. You can change this code, but you must be very careful not to add spaces or new characters by accident.[2] Use the left and right arrow keys to move in the text box.

<hr>

2 To learn more about the code for Superflat preset worlds, visit the official Minecraft Wikipedia site at minecraft.gamepedia.com and search for "superflat."

10. Make the following changes:

- Change **5*minecraft:stone** to **45*minecraft:stone**.
- Change **90*minecraft:water** to **15*minecraftwater**. This will allow shipwrecks to be reachable from the surface.
- Change **deep_ocean** to **lukewarm_ocean**. This will prevent ocean monuments from generating.
- Change **biome_1** to **biome_1,decoration** with no spaces. This will allow decorative blocks like kelp to generate with the biome.

Your new code should now read:

minecraft:bedrock,45*minecraft:stone,5*minecraft:dirt,5*minecraft:sand,15*minecraft:water;minecraft:lukewarm_ocean;oceanmonument,biome_1,decoration (again, with no spaces). Click Use Preset.

Select a Preset

Want to share your preset with someone? Use the below box!

t:water;minecraft:lukewarm_ocean;oceanmonument,biome_1,decor|

Alternatively, here's some we made earlier!

Classic Flat

Tunnelers' Dream

Water World

Overworld

Snowy Kingdom

Use Preset   Cancel

11. On the Superflat Customization, you should see your change reflected in the list of layers. Click Done.

12. On the Create New World: More Options screen, click Create New World.

Use a Buffet World

A buffet world is a world that has just one biome, and you can select whichever biome you want from the "buffet" of biomes Minecraft has, from Badlands to Wooded Mountains. You can also choose between three types of world generation: Surface, which is the normal world type with sky above land; Caves, which is a world made entirely of caves; and Floating Islands, which is made entirely of islands floating above the Void. First, follow steps 1 to 3 above to launch Minecraft and select Create a New World and open the More World Options screen.

1. On the More World Options screen, click the World Type button several times to change this to Buffet. Then click the Customize button.

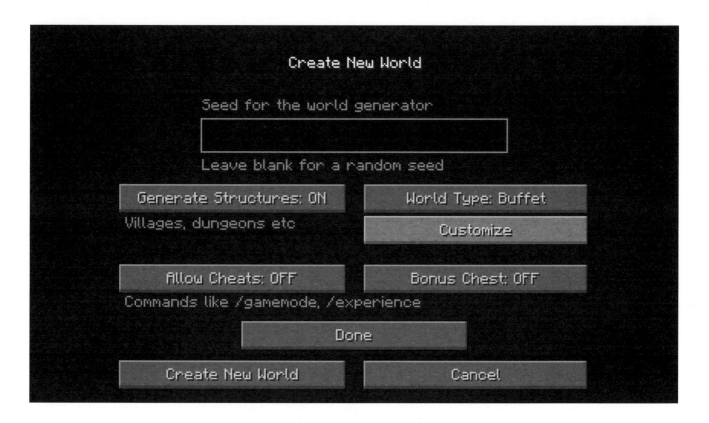

2. On the Buffet world customization screen, select an ocean biome. You may want to avoid Warm Oceans and Frozen Oceans, as these biomes don't have kelp, which can be a good food source. Click Done.

3. On the Create New World screen, click Create New World to launch your new Water World.

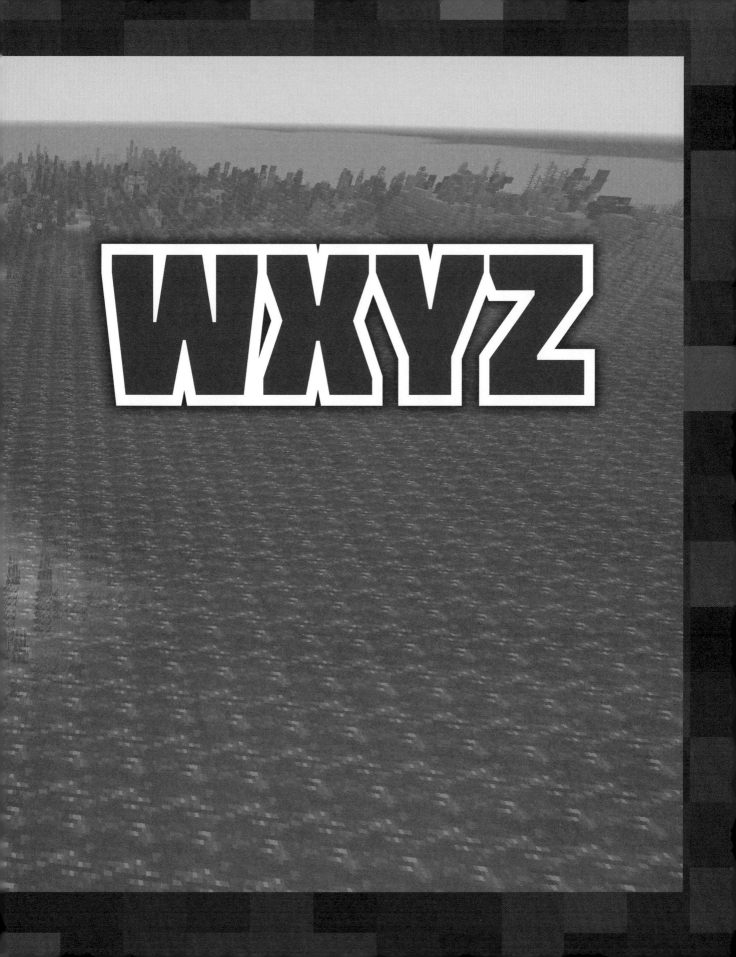

WARM OCEAN

The Warm Ocean Biome has the lightest, greenest waters of all the ocean biomes. The sea floor is made of sand, and sea pickles further light up the biome. The Warm Ocean is the only biome where coral reefs and tropical fish can be found. You will also find pufferfish and seagrass here, along with the occasional underwater ruin (sandstone variants) and shipwrecks.

Deep Warm Oceans do not generate naturally in Minecraft, presumably because some or much of their warmth comes also from being shallow: shallow waters heat up more quickly from the sun than do deeper waters. However, the Deep Warm Ocean is in the game—you can specify it as a biome with a Superflat or Buffet world.

See also: Biomes; Biomes, Aquatic.

WATER

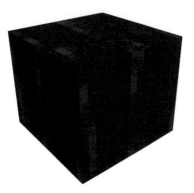

Water is a widespread block that is generated in Minecraft's Overworld to create lakes, oceans, rivers, springs*, and wells. Water is possibly the most unusual and complex block in Minecraft. It can flow (or spread), be picked up and replaced by buckets, and be placed in cauldrons.

Water source blocks are full block areas occupied by water. If an empty block is next to a water source block, the source block creates flowing water blocks that can spread up to seven blocks further, and more if the terrain lowers. Players and mobs can be pushed by a flowing water current, and this feature is often used in mob farms to move entities to a killing chamber.

Water can be moved through, by wading in shallow water or swimming, and allows different speeds of movement, depending on any currents (flowing water), sprint-swimming, swimming down or up or turning, depth, and status effects. Underwater, players will have a slower mining speed and limited visibility. Light levels reduce by one level for each block of water above a block.

Other features that make water an unusual block are that it damages mobs and players through drowning damage, can be soaked up by dry sponges, and turns concrete powder into concrete.

Additionally, the color of water changes from biome to biome: water in warmer oceans is lighter and more greenish than in cold oceans, whose blues darken and deepen with lower temperatures. In swamps, the water changes to a murky brownish green.

See also: Swimming, Waterlogging, Items Float.

* Springs are those single blocks of water you find on mountains that flow down the mountainside.

WATERLOGGING

Waterlogging is a characteristic of some non-solid blocks that allows them to occupy the same space with a water source. That water source remains even when that block is broken. This allows objects like fences and walls to be placed in water without creating an awkward break in the water blocks surrounding them. Currently, the types of blocks that are waterloggable include aquatic flora and fauna, chests, fences, glass panes, iron bars, item frames, ladders, signs, slabs, stairs, trapdoors, and walls.

YELLOW TANG

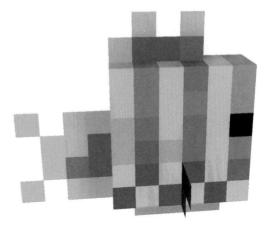

The yellow tang is one of Minecraft's twenty-two tropical fish named for a real-life fish. In Minecraft's color and pattern scheme, it is a yellow stripey. Real-world yellow tangs are part of the tang family of fish and are known for cleaning up ocean turtle's shells by nibbling algae from them.

See also: Black Tang, Blue Tang, Tropical Fish.

YELLOWTAIL PARROTFISH

The yellowtail parrotfish (in BE, the yellowtail parrot) is one of the twenty-two tropical fish in Minecraft that

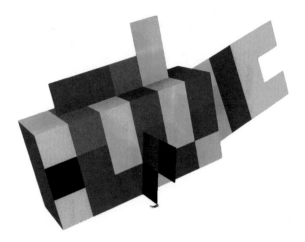

are named for a real-life fish. In Minecraft's color and pattern scheme, the yellowtail parrotfish is a teal-yellow dasher. Yellowtail parrotfish in the real world, also known as redfin parrotfish, are members of the parrotfish family, named for their beak-like mouths. They can grow to over 1 foot long and are a food fish in the Caribbean.

See also: Parrotfish, Tropical Fish.